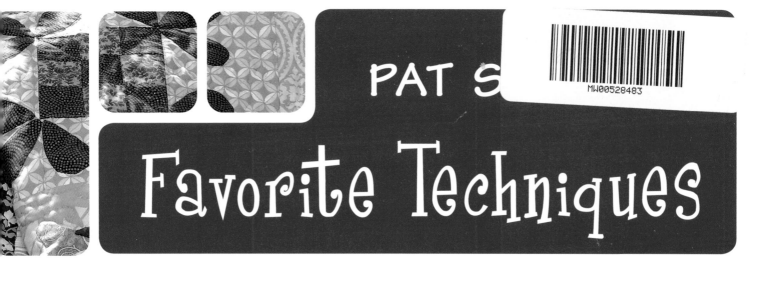

PAT S
Favorite Techniques

Do you know the very best thing about quilts? There are hundreds of ways to make them!

In fact, I sometimes think the only difficult part of our craft is just deciding what kind of quilt to make next. Many of my books are written with this wonderful dilemma in mind. In the last few years, I've covered everything from making your very first quilt to choosing fabric colors and how to do a "round robin" project with your friends. This particular book focuses on a few of my favorite techniques. You'll see a selection of quilts made using each method. You'll also see how flexible these techniques really are. From pretty Appliqué to fun Calendar, Trash Bag, and Utility techniques, this book is all about creating your next quilt and enjoying every minute of it!

-Pat

LEISURE ARTS, INC.
Little Rock, Arkansas

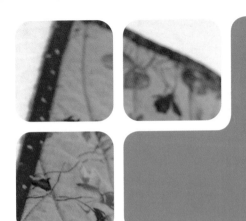

Table of Contents

EDITORIAL STAFF
Managing Editor: Susan White Sullivan
Designer Relations Director: Debra Nettles
Senior Prepress Director: Mark Hawkins
Quilt Publications Director: Cheryl Johnson
Art Publications Director: Rhonda Shelby
Technical Editor: Lisa Lancaster
Technical Writer: Jean Lewis
Editorial Writer: Susan McManus Johnson
Special Projects Director: Susan Frantz Wiles
Art Category Manager: Lora Puls
Graphic Artists: Amy Temple and
    Frances Huddleston
Imaging Technicians: Brian Hall,
    Stephanie Johnson, and Mark R. Potter
Photography Manager: Katherine Atchison
Photography Stylists: Cassie Francioni and
    Sondra Daniel
Staff Photographer: Lloyd Litsey
Contributing Photographer: Jason Masters
Publishing Systems Administrator:
    Becky Riddle
Publishing Systems Assistants: Clint Hanson
    and John Rose.

BUSINESS STAFF
Vice President and Chief Operations Officer:
    Tom Siebenmorgen
Corporate Planning and Development Director:
    Laticia Mull Dittrich
Vice President, Sales and Marketing:
    Pam Stebbins
National Accounts Director: Martha Adams
Sales and Services Director: Margaret Reinold
Information Technology Director: Hermine Linz
Controller: Laura Ogle
Vice President, Operations: Jim Dittrich
Comptroller, Operations: Rob Thieme
Retail Customer Service Manager: Stan Raynor
Print Production Manager: Fred F. Pruss.

Library of Congress Catalog Number: 2008929075

ISBN-13: 978-1-60140-683-5
ISBN-10: 1- 60140-683-5

10 9 8 7 6 5 4 3 2 1

Want to know anything about quilts? Just ask Pat Sloan. Or attend her workshop. Or get one of her books.

Want to stump Pat Sloan? Ask her about her hobbies.

"Well," she says after a long pause and a chuckle, "I like to garden. But really, my life is all about quilting, twenty-four/seven."

"Our time to just relax happens while my husband and I travel for work," the Virginia resident says. "Gregg and I drive to most of our workshops and lectures because of all the quilts and equipment we bring along. We meet the nicest people and get to see lots of new places that are within a day's drive from home.

"I've been fulltime at this career since 2000. Gregg does the management, shipping, ordering, accounting, wrangling the quilts and the sound equipment—keeping me free to teach, lecture, and do the creative side."

> "I like to garden.
> But really, my life is all about
> quilting, twenty-four/seven."

And create, she does! Allocating her at-home time between drawing patterns and developing fabrics, Pat still finds time to update her Web site. Visitors to QuiltersHome.com can read her blog, subscribe to her newsletter, and check for workshops in their area. They'll also find a variety of publications, patterns, notions, and Pat's popular fabric lines from P&B Textiles, all available for purchase. There are even a few freebie patterns just for inspiration.

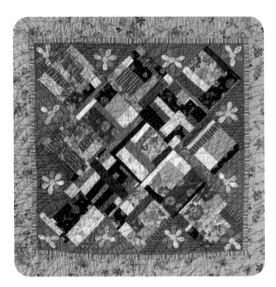

With their business doing so well, you might think that the Sloans would be ready to just sit back and take it easy now and then. Instead, Gregg and Pat have found a way to take their work with them on vacation. They've recently added quilting cruises to their schedule of events, with Pat teaching up to 50 students between ports of call.

In an affectionate salute to their favorite designer, Pat's most devoted fans call themselves "Sloanies." To get a peek into one of the reasons why she's so admired, take a look at her energetic (yet lovely) fabrics, whimsical patterns, and friendly publications: Pat knows that today's quilters want to enjoy themselves while they learn. And if there's anyone who can take the fun craft of quilting and make it downright exhilarating, it's Pat Sloan.

Appliqué Basics

I love appliqué! Unlike piecing, where you have to worry about being precise and matching points, appliqué gives you the freedom to create, adjust, and change the design as you desire. Hand appliqué is portable and relaxing. Machine appliqué lets you quickly add flowers and other shapes to your quilts to make them more interesting.

Whether you are planning to try Mock Hand, Needleturn, or Running Stitch Appliqué, the topics in **Appliqué Basics**, pages 6- 11, can be used with any appliqué technique. Your project instructions will refer you to any information that is specific to that technique.

Selecting Fabric

I really enjoy digging into my fabric collection to find just the right fabrics to make my appliqué shapes SING! So I want to share some of my Tips and Hints for taking your appliqué projects up a notch by using exciting and unusual prints.

Fig. 1

- First, don't think about the PATTERN on the fabric — just think COLOR. For example, if you want to appliqué a blue bird, pull together an assortment of blue fabrics. Be sure to include some florals, fabrics with images (like moons or stars), plaids, checks, stripes, and dots (**Fig. 1**).

- Now look at the fabrics. Do you have a variety of print sizes? Depending on the size of your bird, you might want to choose some even larger scale prints to try.

- To help you visualize how different fabrics will look as a bird appliqué, you can create a shape "window". Make a copy of the pattern, cut out the shape, and then lay the remaining paper on your fabric. Try this with several of your fabrics until you find one that pleases you (**Fig. 2**).

- When using large scale or spotty prints you don't want too many areas on the edges of the shape that are very similar to the color of your background. That will cause you to lose the shape into the background. If this happens, try another fabric with less of your background color or one with a smaller print.

- My last tip is to HAVE FUN!!! Try using a huge floral for a house, a stripe for a roof, or a polka dot for leaves (**Fig. 3**). Your whimsical nature will help you create an awesome quilt; you just need to trust it. The more you use fabrics with pattern, the more comfortable you will become picking the right fabric for your appliqués. And…once you start using these fun fabrics, you won't be able to stop!

Fig. 2

Fig. 3

Want to learn more?

For more in-depth color studies and to learn more about how I look at color in fabric check out my book *Take The Fear Out Of Color*, Leisure Arts leaflet #4286.

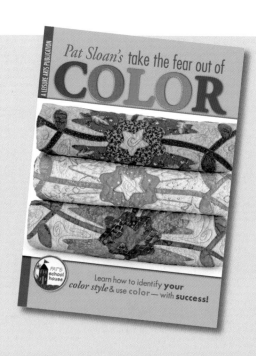

Making Bias Tape

To make stems and vines, I like to use a bias tape maker. I not only make what I need for my current project—I make oodles of stems to have handy for future projects! I roll the extra onto empty toilet paper rolls (oh yes, they do have a use) and keep the rolls in a basket, ready to use as needed.

Fig. 4

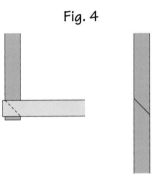

1. Refer to the manufacturer's instructions for the correct width to cut your bias strips. Cut enough strips to make the total (or more!) length needed.
2. If needed to obtain desired length, use the diagonal seams method to sew strips together to make one long strip. (**Fig. 4**).
3. Place strip right side down on an ironing board. Insert point of strip into wide end of bias tape maker (**Fig. 5**).
4. Use a pin to help feed the strip into the bias tape maker while slowly sliding the tape maker down the strip (**Fig. 6**). The long raw edges will turn inward as the tape maker slides. When you have about an inch of bias tape showing, pin the point to ironing board. (**Fig. 7**).
5. With the tip of your iron, press the folded edges flat as you continue sliding and pressing along the entire length of the strip (**Figs. 8-9**).

Fig. 5

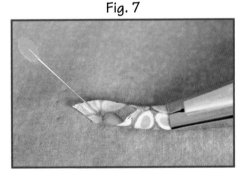

Fig. 6

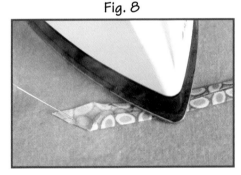

Fig. 7

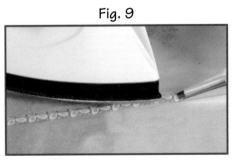

Fig. 8

Fig. 9

Finished Bias Tape

Painting the Appliqué "Picture"

To me a quilt is a "picture" and before I start stitching the appliqués in place, I need to arrange ALL the pieces of the picture on the background to check placement. I also want to be sure I am satisfied with my fabric choices and the shape of the pieces. (Yes, you can change the shape of an appliqué if you don't like it!).

- Refer to your pattern's Quilt Top Diagram or photo when arranging the appliqués on your background.

- To make placement lines for symmetrical designs, fold your background piece in half lengthwise, crosswise and diagonally; lightly press folds. Unfold and use the creases as placement guides.

- I usually place the largest shapes first. When satisfied with their placement, I tuck stems and leaves under the edges of large flowers and chimneys under roof edges, etc. This gives me more control over the spacing of shapes (**Fig. 10**).

- With some designs you may find it easier to place the shapes closest to the background first and work upward to "stack" or layer the appliqués (**Figs. 11-12**).

- For large quilts I like to spread the background out on the floor to arrange the appliqué shapes. If you don't have a large area (or just don't want to crawl on the floor!), you might look for a place where you can push two tables together, such as a church, school, library, or community center to use when laying out your quilt.

- If the quilt is VERY large you may want to arrange, baste, and then appliqué it in sections or blocks. You can assemble the sections or blocks into a quilt top after the stitching is finished.

Fig. 10

Fig. 11

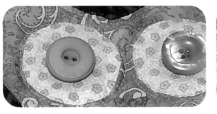

Fig. 12

- If you plan to assemble your quilt in sections and it has shapes that extend into other blocks or the borders, arrange them as they will appear on the finished project, allowing the parts of the shapes that extend to hang off the background. **Note:** After you have basted and appliquéd the parts of the shapes that are actually on the background, you will finish piecing the quilt top and then baste and appliqué the extended parts of the shapes.

- When painting a Needleturn or Running Stitch Appliqué picture, check to be sure that when you turn under the seam allowance of the shapes ON TOP the appliqué covers the raw edges of the shapes below, such as stem ends. It's maddening to have a shape almost stitched and discover it does not quite cover a raw edge below.

- When you need to make multiples of a block, arrange one complete block first. Then, refer to the completed block as you work to help keep the remaining blocks uniform.

Once you have painted your appliqué picture it's time to baste the pieces to the background.

Basting

All of my basting is done with BASTING GLUE, yeah! No dealing with pins, no stitching… just nice, easy to use basting glue. If you are not familiar with this product, there are several brands available. My favorite is Roxanne's™ Glue-Baste-It™.

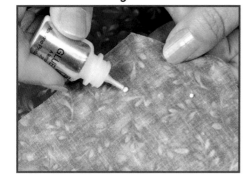

Fig. 13

- The most important thing you need to know when glue basting is that it only takes a tiny line or tiny dots of glue to hold a shape in place (**Fig. 13**).

- Some basting glue bottles have a "snip off" top. If that is the type you have, I suggest you DO NOT snip off the top (the hole is always too big). Instead, take off the cap, pour a small amount into a container, and use a toothpick to place dots. Not as handy, but it does work.

- When basting a single shape, I apply a few drops of glue to the wrong side of the shape (**Fig. 14**), then press it firmly in place on the background (**Fig. 15**).

- When basting stems, I lay a THIN line of glue on the *background* where I plan to place the stem. Then I put the stem on top of the glue line. This is MUCH easier than pinning a stem, then lifting it to glue under it (believe me, I did that for years!).

tip Basting glue dries quickly, so if you are working with long stems or vines, like you may find on borders, I recommend working in sections. For example, apply the glue to one border at a time or even just ½ of the border.

- When basting stacked or overlapping shapes, I begin with the shapes closest to the background. I lift a small section of each appliqué and place several tiny drops of glue on the wrong side (**Fig. 16**), then press firmly in place on background. Continue lifting and pressing until you have basted the entire picture.

Fig. 14

Fig. 15

Fig. 16

Choosing the Right Thread

- I usually choose a color that matches the appliqué but sometimes I will use a shade of brown or gray because they blend so well.

- When selecting thread color, always lay a single strand of the thread on the appliqué fabric. The denseness of thread on a spool makes it hard to tell if it is a good match (**Fig. 17**).

- Since you will rarely find a "perfect match", pick a thread color that is slightly DARKER than your appliqué fabric. Remember that light colors come forward and dark ones recede.

Fig. 17

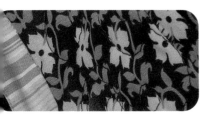

11

Mock Hand Appliqué

When I want the smooth-edged, turned-under look of traditional Needleturn Appliqué but the speed of machine appliqué, this is the method I like to use. When viewed from a distance, the machine Blind Hem Stitch I use around the appliqué shapes really looks like hand appliqué! Also, I like the fact that there is no fraying around the edges of the appliqués when the quilt is washed.

Supplies

In addition to my fabric and basic sewing supplies, there are a few special supplies I use when doing Mock Hand Appliqué.

- **Heat-resistant Template Plastic** – I prefer Templar® brand. It is lightly frosted but clear enough to see through when tracing patterns. It also cuts easily with utility scissors or a rotary cutter.

- **Starch** – I use Mary Ellen's Best Press™ but any brand of spray starch will work. I like Best Press™ because it does not leave a flakey residue, comes in liquid form, and is available in several yummy fragrances.

- **Small Cup** – I find that a small medicine cup or large bottle cap works well to hold the starch.

- **Basting Glue** – I like Roxanne's™ Glue-Baste-It™. It is 100% water-soluble, but for those projects that won't be washed, it does not feel stiff when dry. It is available in a handy travel size bottle (.25 ounce) with a syringe applicator that allows for the controlled placement of the glue drops.

- **Paintbrush** – I use a small inexpensive craft paintbrush to apply the starch.

- **Sewing Machine Needles** – I usually use a size 70 multi-purpose needle with great success. If you have trouble with skipped or uneven stitches, try a Sharp or Quilting needle in a size 60 or 70.

- **Open Toe Presser Foot** – It is very important to be able to see where you are stitching. I suggest that you check with your sewing machine manufacturer for one designed for your machine.

- **Thread** – I usually use 60 weight 100% cotton thread in a color that matches the appliqué. Mettler® Silk-Finish and Aurifil™ Cotton Makó™ are two of my favorites. See **Choosing the Right Thread**, page 11, to learn more about selecting thread color.

Making and Using Templates

The Mock Hand Appliqué patterns in this book are printed in reverse.
They are the reverse of the finished appliqués on the quilt.

1. To make a template from a pattern, lay your template plastic over the pattern and use a fine-point permanent marker or pen to carefully trace the pattern (**Fig. 1**).

Fig. 1

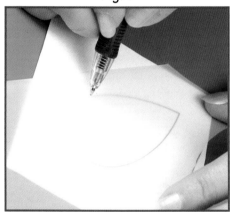

tip When working with larger shapes that have sharp points or deep V's, you can round the points or V's a bit when tracing the templates. By doing so the points or V's are not as challenging to turn under when preparing and appliquéing the shapes. You can even REDRAW the shape if you choose—oh yes you can! Nice to have freedom of choice!

2. Cut out the template on the drawn line. Cut as smoothly as you can. If your template edges have bumps, so will your finished appliqué shape.

3. Repeat Steps 1 and 2 to make a template for each different appliqué in your project instructions.

tip Because the starched fabric will need to dry completely before removing the template for re-use, cutting multiple templates of the same shape will help to speed the pressing process in **Preparing The Appliqués**, page 14.

tip While heat-resistant template plastic is designed to be used over and over again, sometimes it will warp after being used multiple times. If my project instructions call for a large number of appliqués of the same shape, I usually make several templates of that shape.

tip Keeping in mind that you will be drawing around the templates onto the fabric with the reverse side facing up, just as you traced the pattern, you might find it helpful to mark the side of the template that will be facing up. You could write "this side up" or even just a WS for Wrong Side.

4. Place the template, marked side up, on the WRONG SIDE of your fabric. Using a fine-point wash out marker, chalk pencil, or fabric marking pencil, draw around the shape. Leaving at least 1/2" between shapes, draw the number of shapes called for in the instructions for each fabric.

5. Leaving about a 1/4" seam allowance, cut out the shape. Don't cut too closely to the drawn line; you can always trim your seam allowance later if needed.

6. Repeat Steps 4 and 5 to draw and cut out all of the appliqué shapes called for in the project instructions.

tip I like to cut out all the shapes and then arrange them on a flat surface or my design wall, as they will be placed on the quilt. By doing this, I can see that I have all the pieces I need before moving to the ironing board to prepare them. Also, I can be sure that my fabric choices work well together.

tip You may want to cut a few extra shapes to use for practice when Preparing The Appliqués. For most of us, it takes a while to get into the rhythm of turning under the edges smoothly.

Preparing the Appliqués

Fig. 2

Fig. 3

Fig. 4

1. Set your iron on "cotton". Do not use steam.
2. Pour or spray a small amount of starch into your cup or bottle cap. **Note:** Aerosol starches will foam up when sprayed. That's ok, you can dip your brush into the foam and use it, or you can wait until the foam turns to liquid.
3. With the wrong side of the fabric facing up, center your template, marked side up, inside the marked lines of your fabric shape. Using your brush, apply a heavy coat of starch in the seam allowance around the entire shape (**Fig. 2**). Do one shape at a time and saturate the seam allowance with starch.
4. Hold the template firmly in place with your fingertips. Starting on the longest flat side, use the tip of your iron to turn and press the seam allowance over the edge of the template (**Fig. 3**).

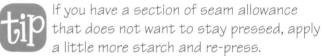 If you have a section of seam allowance that does not want to stay pressed, apply a little more starch and re-press.

5. Referring to **Pretty Points** and **Incredible Innies**, as needed, continue turning and pressing until the entire seam allowance is pressed in place. Allow piece to dry completely.
6. Repeat Steps 1-5 for each appliqué shape in your project.
7. Carefully remove the templates (**Fig. 4**). Repress seam allowances, if needed.

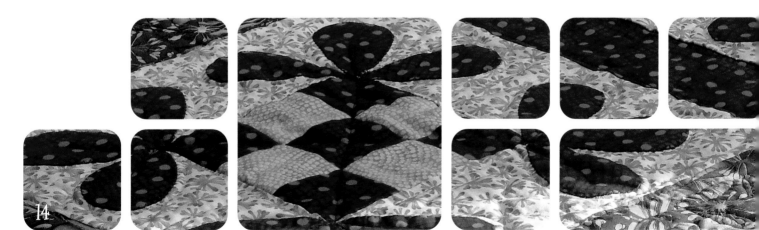

Pretty Points

- If your shape has an outward point, like the tip of a leaf, stop turning and pressing about 1" from the point.

- Fold the point of the fabric perpendicular to point of the template and press in place. Go back and finish turning and pressing the original side (**Fig. 5**).

- Fold the second side over the template to give the appliqué a nice sharp point and press (**Fig. 6**).

Fig. 5 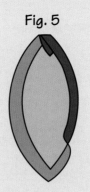 **Fig. 6**

Incredible Innies

- If your shape has an inward "V", at the point of the V, clip the seam allowance right up to the drawn line (**Fig. 7**).

- Starting on one long flat side of the V, use the tip of your iron to turn and press the seam allowance over the template, stopping about one inch from the point. Repeat on the other side.

- Now, fold over BOTH sides to the point and press in place. There will be very little seam allowance at the point to turn over the template (**Fig. 8**).

Fig. 7 **Fig. 8**

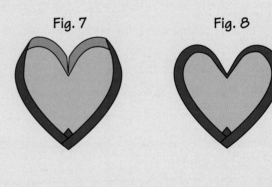

tip The steeper the V, the less seam allowance there is to turn under as you reach the point. Do not over work or over press the point of the V.

Before stitching, I like to arrange all my shapes on my background. Refer to **Painting the Appliqué Picture**, page 9, for details.

The Mock Hand Appliqué Stitch

The stitch I use for Mock Hand Appliqué has several different names depending on your brand of machine. It is often called a Blind Hem Stitch. The important thing is that you want a stitch that looks like this ⅄⅄⅄, with a TINY bite (⅄) and very few straight stitches BETWEEN the bites.

MACHINE SET UP

1. Thread your sewing machine and bobbin with 100% cotton thread.
2. Attach an open-toe presser foot. Select needle down (if your machine has this feature).
3. Find the stitch on your machine that most closely resembles my stitch (**Fig. 9**) and sew some test samples.
4. If your stitch does not look like mine, try one or more of the following:
   - If your stitch has several straight stitches between the bites that make the bites far apart, try shortening the stitch length. If the bites are still not close enough to make a pretty stitch on small pieces you may still be able to use it for larger shapes.
   - If your bite is too deep, try shortening the stitch width. If you feel your bite is still too deep, try using a lighter weight thread.
   - If your machine doesn't have a stitch that looks anything like mine, or if none of the solutions above work, you could just select another decorative stitch such as a blanket or zigzag. Or mmm…maybe it's time for a new machine!

So you have selected your stitch and done a test sample. Great! Time to sew.

STITCHING

Note: For photography purposes I used a contrasting thread. You will want to use a matching thread for your project.

 I like to work from the bottom layer up, stitching the appliqués that are closest to the background first. I feel it helps keep the shapes flat.

Fig. 9

Fig. 10

 I try to stitch as much as I can with the same color thread before changing to the next color. For example, I try to stitch all of the stems and leaves with the same green. Then all the red berries with the same red…etc.

1. Bring bobbin thread to the top of the fabric by lowering then raising the needle, bringing up the bobbin thread loop. Pull the loop all the way to the surface.
2. Begin by stitching 5 or 6 stitches in place (drop feed dogs or set stitch length at 0), or use your machine's lock stitch feature, if equipped, to anchor thread. Return setting to selected stitch.
3. The bite of the stitch should be done on the appliqué with the straight stitches falling onto the background at the very outside edge of the appliqué (**Fig. 10**).

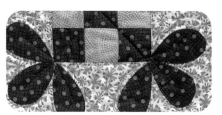

4. (*Note:* Dots on **Figs. 11 – 15** indicate where to leave needle in fabric when pivoting.) Always stop with needle down in background fabric. Refer to **Fig. 10** to stitch outside points, like the tips of leaves. Stop one stitch short of point. Raise presser foot. Pivot project slightly, lower presser foot, and make **Stitch 1**. Take next stitch, stop at point, and pivot to make **Stitch 2**. Pivot slightly to make **Stitch 3**. Continue stitching.

5. For outside corners (**Fig. 12**) stitch to corner, stopping with needle in background fabric. Raise presser foot. Pivot project, lower presser foot take 1 angled stitch. Pivot and stitch adjacent side.

6. For inside corners (**Fig. 13**), stitch to the corner, taking the last bite at corner and stopping with the needle down in background fabric. Raise presser foot. Pivot project, lower presser foot take 1 angled stitch. Pivot and stitch adjacent side.

7. When stitching outside curves (**Fig. 14**), stop with needle down in background fabric. Raise presser foot and pivot project as needed. Lower presser foot and continue stitching, pivoting as often as necessary to follow curve. Small circles may require pivoting between each stitch.

8. When stitching inside curves (**Fig. 15**), stop with needle down in background fabric. Raise presser foot and pivot project as needed. Lower presser foot and continue stitching, pivoting as often as necessary to follow curve.

9. To finish, use a lock stitch to sew 5 or 6 stitches in place or use a needle to pull threads to wrong side of background fabric (**Fig. 16**); knot, then trim ends.

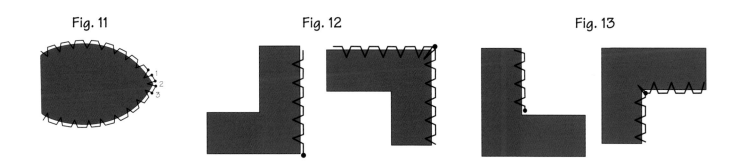

Fig. 11   Fig. 12   Fig. 13

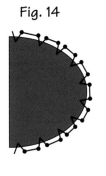      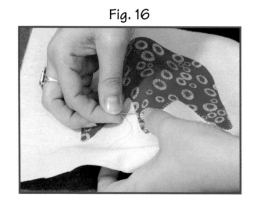

Fig. 14   Fig. 15   Fig. 16

17

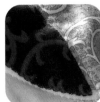

Owl and Honey Bee Quilt

I have a love of owls that goes back to the collection I started in high school! I just love their big eyes and little roly-poly shapes. But the best thing for me is getting to see a REAL owl!

For this quilt I alternated appliquéd Owl blocks with the pieced and appliquéd Honey Bee blocks. For added interest I made the blocks different widths and used buttons for the eyes.

Finished Quilt Size: 42" x 44½" (107 cm x 113 cm)
Finished Honey Bee Block A Size: 13" x 10½" (33 cm x 27 cm)
Finished Honey Bee Block B Size: 10½" x 10½" (27 cm x 27 cm)
Finished Owl Block Size: 8" x 10½" (20 cm x 27 cm)

FABRIC REQUIREMENTS

Yardage is based on 43"/44" (109 cm/112 cm) wide fabric. Refer to **Selecting Fabric**, page 6, for my tips on choosing fabrics for your appliqués.

- ⅜ yd (34 cm) of green print No. 1
- ½ yd (46 cm) of green print No. 2
- ⅜ yd (34 cm) of green floral
- ¼ yd (23 cm) of green stripe
- 1⅝ yds (1.5 m) of blue print No. 1 (includes binding)
- ⅜ yd (34 cm) of blue print No. 2
- ¼ yd (23 cm) of blue print No. 3
- ⅛ yd (11 cm) of tan print No. 1
- ¼ yd (23 cm) **each** of tan prints No. 2 and No. 3
- 8" x 15" (20 cm x 38 cm) rectangle of cream print
- 6" x 6" (15 cm x 15 cm) square of orange print
- 2¾ yds (2.5 m) of backing fabric

You will also need:

- 46" x 48½" (117 cm x 123 cm) rectangle of batting
- 10 green 1" (25 mm) diameter buttons
- See **Supplies**, page 12, for my list of special Mock Hand Appliqué supplies

CUTTING THE BACKGROUND AND BORDERS

Follow **Rotary Cutting**, page 103, to cut fabric. Cut all strips from the selvage-to-selvage width of the fabric unless otherwise noted. All measurements include ¼" seam allowances.

From green print No. 1:
- Cut 2 **rectangles** 8½" x 11".

From green print No. 2:
- Cut 1 strip 3½" wide. From this strip, cut 8 **small rectangles** 5" x 3½".
- Cut 1 strip 11" wide. From this strip, cut 4 **medium rectangles** 3½" x 11" and 4 **large rectangles** 4¾" x 11".

From green floral:
- Cut 3 **rectangles** 8½" x 11".

From green stripe:
- Cut 2 **top/bottom middle borders** 1½" x 31½".
- Cut 2 **side middle borders** 1½" x 36".

CUTTING THE BACKGROUND AND BORDERS (continued)

From blue print No. 1:
- Cut 2 lengthwise **top/bottom inner borders** 1½" x 29½".
- Cut 2 lengthwise **side inner borders** 1½" x 34".
- Cut 2 lengthwise **top/bottom outer borders** 4½" x 33½".
- Cut 2 lengthwise **side outer borders** 4½" x 44".
- Cut 5 **binding strips** 1½" wide.

From blue print No. 2:
- Cut 2 strips 2" wide. From these strips, cut 2 **long strips** 2" x 20" and 1 **short strip** 2" x 10".

From tan print No. 1:
- Cut 1 strip 2" wide. From this strip, cut 1 **long strip** 2" x 20" and 2 **short strips** 2" x 10".

CUTTING THE APPLIQUÉS

*Follow **Making and Using Templates**, page 13, to cut and prepare appliqués using patterns, page 23.*

From blue print No. 2:
- Cut 36 **bees**.

From blue print No. 3:
- Cut 12 **bees**.
- Cut 5 **wings**; cut 5 **wings reversed**.
- Cut 5 **topknots**.

From tan print No. 2:
- Cut 3 **owls**.

From tan print No. 3:
- Cut 2 **owls**.

From cream print:
- Cut 10 **eyes**.

From orange print:
- Cut 5 **beaks**.

MAKING THE HONEY BEE BLOCKS

*Follow **Piecing**, page 103, and **Pressing**, page 104, to assemble the blocks. Use ¼" seam allowances throughout.*

1. Sew 2 **blue print No. 2 long strips** and 1 **tan print No. 1 long strip** together to make **Strip Set A**. Cut across Strip Set A at 2" intervals to make 8 **Unit 1's**.

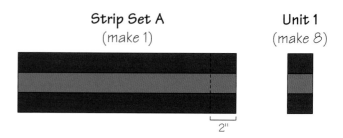

Strip Set A (make 1)   **Unit 1** (make 8)

2. Sew 2 **tan print No. 1 short strips** and 1 **blue print No. 2 short strip** together to make **Strip Set B**. Cut across Strip Set B at 2" intervals to make 4 **Unit 2's**.

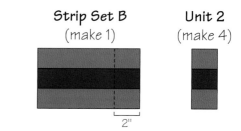

Strip Set B (make 1)   **Unit 2** (make 4)

3. Sew 2 **Units 1** and 1 **Unit 2** together to make **Nine-Patch Unit**. Make 4 Nine-Patch Units.

Nine-Patch Unit (make 4)

4. Sew **green print No. 2 small rectangles** to opposite sides of a Nine-Patch Unit. Sew 1 **green print No. 2 large rectangle** to each remaining side to make **Honey Bee Block A**. Make 2 Honey Bee Block A's.

Honey Bee Block A (make 2)

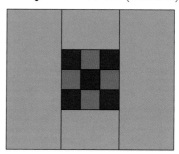

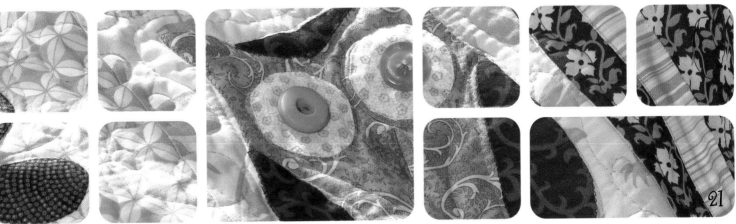

21

5. Sew 2 **green print No. 2 small rectangles** to opposite sides of a Nine-Patch Unit. Sew 1 **green print No. 2 medium rectangle** to each remaining side to make **Honey Bee Block B**. Make 2 Honey Bee Block B's.

Honey Bee Block B (make 2)

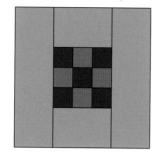

ADDING THE APPLIQUÉS

Refer to **Appliqué Basics**, page 6, to prepare your project for stitching. Refer to photo, page 21, for placement. Follow **The Mock Hand Appliqué Stitch**, page 16, for technique.

1. Appliqué 12 **bees** to each Honey Bee Block.
2. Appliqué 1 **owl**, 1 **wing**, 1 **wing reversed**, 1 **topknot**, 2 **eyes**, and 1 **beak** to each **green print No. 1** and **green floral rectangle** to make 5 Owl Blocks.

Owl Block (make 5)

ASSEMBLING THE QUILT TOP CENTER

1. Sew 1 Honey Bee Block A and 2 Owl Blocks together to make **Row A**. Make 2 Row A's.
2. Sew 1 Owl and 2 Honey Bee Block B's together to make **Row B**. Make 1 Row B.
3. Sew rows together to make **quilt top center**.
4. Sew **top**, **bottom**, and then **side inner borders** to quilt top center.
5. Sew **top**, **bottom**, and then **side middle borders** to quilt top center.
6. Sew **top**, **bottom**, and then **side outer borders** to quilt top center.

FINISHING THE QUILT

1. Follow **Quilting**, page 106, to mark, layer, and quilt. My quilt is quilted with outline quilting around the appliqués and middle border. There is an X through the center of the Nine-Patch Units. The block backgrounds are quilted with an allover loop design. There is a wavy line through the center of the inner border and loops in the outer border.
2. Refer to **Making a Hanging Sleeve**, page 109, to make and attach a hanging sleeve, if desired.
3. Use **binding strips** and follow **Pat's Machine-Sewn Binding**, page 110, to bind quilt.
4. Sew one button to the center of each eye.

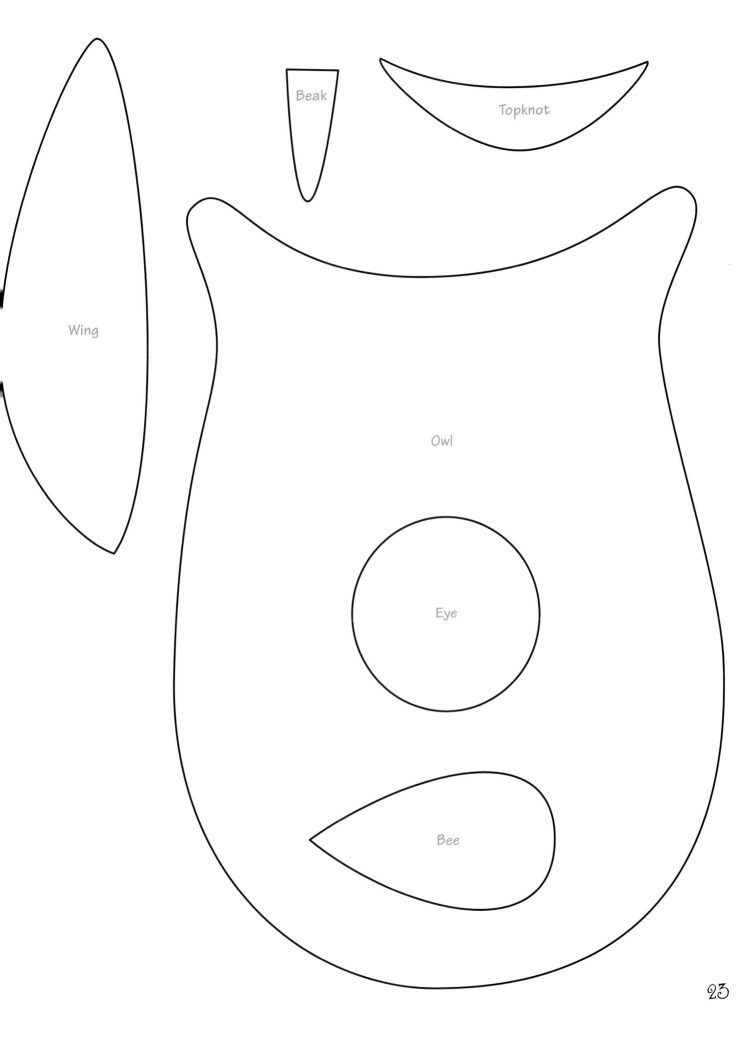

Beak

Topknot

Wing

Owl

Eye

Bee

23

Honey Bee and Dragonfly Table Runner

The traditional Honey Bee block is perfect for learning Mock Hand Appliqué. Its simple design is fast to construct and lets you showcase some of your favorite fabrics (like the cute dragonfly print in the border). Simply make three blocks, add two sashing strips, a border, and binding and you'll have a versatile table runner you can use for any occasion!

Finished Quilt Size: 17¹/₂" x 42¹/₂" (44 cm x 108 cm)
Finished Block Size: 10¹/₂" x 10¹/₂" (27 cm x 27 cm)

FABRIC REQUIREMENTS

*Yardage is based on 43"/44" (109 cm/112 cm) wide fabric. Refer to **Selecting Fabric**, page 6, for my tips on choosing fabrics for your appliqués.*

- ¹/₂ yd (46 cm) of purple print (includes binding)
- ¹/₈ yd (11 cm) of gold print
- ³/₈ yd (34 cm) of light green print
- ³/₈ yd (34 cm) of dark green print
- 1³/₈ yds (1.3 m) of backing fabric

You will also need:

- 21¹/₂" x 46¹/₂" (55 cm x 118 cm) rectangle of batting
- See **Supplies**, page 12, for my list of special Mock Hand Appliqué supplies

CUTTING THE BACKGROUND AND BORDERS

*Follow **Rotary Cutting**, page 103, to cut fabric. Cut all strips from the selvage-to-selvage width of the fabric. All measurements include ¹/₄" seam allowances.*

From purple print:
- Cut 2 **sashing strips** 2¹/₂" x 11".
- Cut 1 strip 2"w. From this strip, cut 3 **strips** 2" x 13".
- Cut 4 **binding strips** 1¹/₂"w.

From gold print:
- Cut 1 strip 2"w. From this strip, cut 3 **strips** 2" x 13".

From light green print:
- Cut 2 strips 3¹/₂"w. From these strips, cut 6 **large rectangles** 3¹/₂" x 11".
- Cut 1 strip 3¹/₂"w. From this strip, cut 6 **small rectangles** 3¹/₂" x 5".

From dark green print:
- Cut 2 **long borders** 3¹/₂" x 36".
- Cut 2 **short borders** 3¹/₂" x 17".

CUTTING THE APPLIQUÉS

Follow **Making and Using Templates**, page 13, to cut and prepare appliqués using pattern, page 27.

From purple print:
- Cut 36 **bees**.

MAKING THE HONEY BEE BLOCKS

Follow **Piecing**, page 103, and **Pressing**, page 104, to assemble the quilt top. Use ¼" seam allowances throughout. Refer to photo for placement when assembling the quilt top.

1. Sew 2 **purple print strips** and 1 **gold print strip** together to make **Strip Set A**. Cut across Strip Set A at 2" intervals to make 6 **Unit 1's**.

Strip Set A
(make 1)

Unit 1
(make 6)

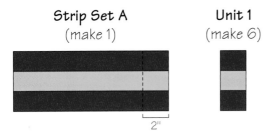

2. Sew 2 **gold print strips** and 1 **purple print strip** together to make **Strip Set B**. Cut across Strip Set B at 2" intervals to make 3 **Unit 2's**.

Strip Set B
(make 1)

Unit 2
(make 3)

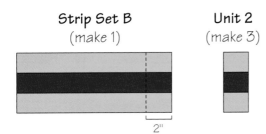

3. Sew 2 **Units 1** and 1 **Unit 2** together to make **Nine-Patch Unit**. Make 3 Nine-Patch Units.

Nine-Patch Unit (make 3)

4. Sew **light green print small rectangles** to opposite sides of a Nine-Patch Unit. Sew 1 **light green print large rectangle** to each remaining side to make **Honey Bee Block**. Make 3 Honey Bee Blocks.

Honey Bee Block (make 3)

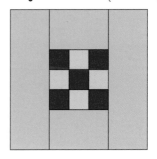

ADDING THE APPLIQUÉS

Refer to **Appliqué Basics**, page 6, to prepare your project for stitching. Follow **The Mock Hand Appliqué Stitch**, page 16, for technique.

1. Appliqué 12 **bees** to each Honey Bee Block.

ASSEMBLING THE TABLE RUNNER TOP

1. Sew 3 Honey Bee Blocks and 2 **sashing strips** together to make **quilt top center**.

Quilt Top Center

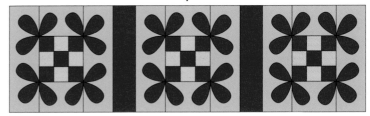

2. Sew **long** and then **short borders** to quilt top center.

FINISHING THE TABLE RUNNER

1. Follow **Quilting**, page 106, to mark, layer, and quilt. My quilt is quilted with outline quilting around the appliqués and an X through the center of the Nine-Patch Units. There is a wavy line across each sashing strip and a leaf and vine pattern in the border.

2. Refer to **Making a Hanging Sleeve**, page 109, to make and attach a hanging sleeve, if desired.

3. Use **binding strips** and follow **Pat's Machine-Sewn Binding**, page 110, to bind quilt.

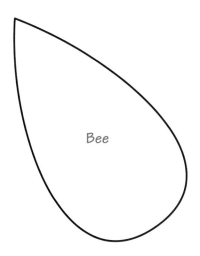

Bee

Needleturn Appliqué

What I enjoy most about any form of hand appliqué is the stitching. With Needleturn Appliqué, you use templates for drawing the appliqué shapes onto fabric but once you cut out the shapes there is very little preparation. This allows me to quickly get to the part I like best — THE STITCHING!

I consider Needleturn to be the most traditional form of hand appliqué. The raw edges of the shapes are turned under with the tip of your needle as you Blindstitch the shapes to the background fabric. If you really love hand stitching I know you'll enjoy this method, too!

Supplies

In addition to my fabric and basic sewing supplies, there are a few special supplies I use when doing Needleturn Appliqué.

- **Template Making Material –** These include Template Plastic, Freezer Paper, or Paper – Refer to **Making And Using Templates**, page 30, for an explanation of the different methods I use when making templates. Once you have chosen your preferred method, select your template material.

- **Fabric Marking Tools –** I like to use a fine- or extra-fine point marking tool when tracing around templates onto fabric. There are many types to choose from. See **Choosing The Right Fabric Marking Tool** to learn more about your choices.

tip When using a dark pen on a light fabric, test your pen on a fabric scrap to be sure the drawn line will not "shadow" through the shape when the line is turned under.

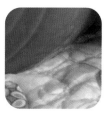

- **Needles** – I like to use #10 or #11 straw needles, which are very long and thin. These needles allow me to take a smaller "bite" of fabric as I stitch. There really is no right or wrong needle for appliqué so I highly recommend that you try several different ones. You may find that you are more comfortable with a shorter needle — use what you like best!

- **Needle Threader** – I love my Clover Desk Needle Threader, it makes threading those small-eye needles a breeze. Simply insert the needle, lay the thread across the threader, and push the button. Remove needle from threader and it's threaded (**Figs. 1-2**)! Why work harder than you need to?

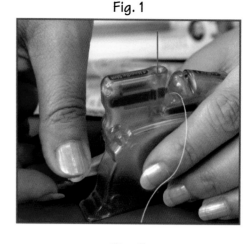
Fig. 1

- **Thread** – I usually use 60-weight 100% cotton thread in a color that matches the appliqué. Mettler® Silk-Finish and Aurifil™ Cotton Makó are two of my favorites. See **Choosing the Right Thread**, page 11, to learn more about choosing the right thread color.

Fig. 2

> **tip** Some people like silk thread because it is very thin. I find it harder to work with because it is slippery, but you might like to give it a try.

- **Thimble** – I prefer a metal or thick leather thimble. I wear it on the middle finger of my right hand (my pushing finger). Because I push the needle through the fabric with the SIDE of my finger, I use a thimble with dimples on the sides. You may find that you push from the top of the thimble. Try stitching with several different thimbles until you find the best one for you.

- **Bias Tape Maker** – Bias tape makers come in a variety of sizes from 1/4" – 2" wide. I use the 1/2" wide size most often. Your project instructions will tell you the size you need. See **Making Bias Tape**, page 8, for more about this handy tool.

Choosing the Right Fabric Marking Tool

My best advice for choosing a marking tool is to use one that allows you to **see** the drawn line. Since you will be turning under the seam allowance AND the drawn line, you can use a marking tool that does not wash out — really!

Chalk Pencil – Works great on dark fabrics. It makes wider line than I normally like, but it's fine for large shapes.

Gel Ink Pens – I love these for use on dark fabrics. Yellow, gold, and peach seem to show up best. I have even used gold metallic – fun!

Lead Pencil – Works on all but the darkest fabrics. You will want to test your pencil to be sure that the line will not smear.

Pigma®Micron® Pens – These make a nice line but I find I have problems with the tip dragging a bit on fabric. You may find that they work great for you!

Water-Soluble Markers – You really don't have to wash the line out, but some people feel more secure knowing that they can.

Ultra Fine-point Sharpies® – These are my favorite. I can see them best, they write nicely and I can use them on all but the darkest fabrics. Since they come in so many colors I can also use them for very light fabrics. I find that I need to keep the pen moving when drawing to avoid a line that bleeds.

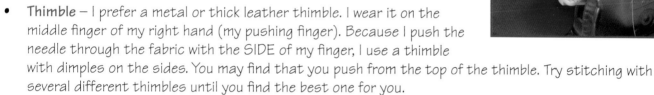

Making and Using Templates

When making your project, you will need to select one of the following methods for making and using templates. If you have never used any of these techniques you may want to try more than one to see which one(s) appeal to you the most.

The Needleturn Appliqué patterns in this book are "right reading". They are printed exactly how they appear on the quilt. If your instructions call for a shape to be reversed it is because it will be used facing both directions.

tip When working with larger shapes that have sharp points or deep V's you can round the points or V's a bit when tracing the templates. By doing that the points or V's are not as challenging to turn under when preparing and appliquéing the shapes. You can even REDRAW the shape if you choose—oh yes you can! Nice to have freedom of choice!

tip Keeping in mind that you will be tracing around the templates onto your fabric with the right side of the templates facing up, you might find it helpful to mark that side with "this side up" or even just a RS for Right Side.

Template Plastic

With this technique you will cut ONE template per shape. So, if you need 15 identical leaves, you will need just ONE template.

1. Lay your template plastic over the pattern and use a fine-point permanent marker or pen to carefully trace the pattern (**Fig. 3**).
2. Cut out the template on the drawn line. Cut as smoothly as you can. If your template edges have bumps, so will your drawn appliqué shape.
3. Repeat Steps 1 and 2 to make ONE template for each different appliqué shape in your project instructions.
4. Place template, marked side up, on the RIGHT SIDE of your fabric. Using a fabric marking tool, draw around the shape (**Fig. 4**). Leaving at least ¹/₂" between shapes, draw the number of shapes called for in the instructions. Repeat for each fabric that uses the shape.
5. Leaving about a ¹/₄" seam allowance, cut out the shapes.

tip When cutting out your appliqué shapes, don't cut too closely to the drawn line. If you find that you have too much bulk when appliquéing, you can trim the seam allowance as you stitch.

6. Repeat Steps 4 and 5 to make all of the appliqué shapes called for in the project instructions.

Fig. 3

Fig. 4

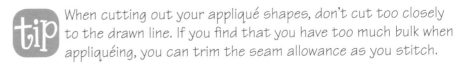

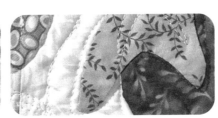

Freezer Paper

Many people prefer to use a template that adheres to and stabilizes the fabric to make tracing around it easier. Freezer paper is perfect for this.

1. Trace the pattern onto the paper (dull) side of freezer paper and cut out. Repeat for each pattern needed.

   tip You can reuse freezer paper templates until they no longer adhere to the fabric, usually four or five times. If you will be using the same shape multiple times, you will want to cut several of that shape.

   tip If you have downloaded a pattern onto your computer, you may be able to print directly from your printer onto freezer paper. I suggest doing a test by cutting an 8½" x 11" sheet of freezer paper, flattening the sheet so that it will feed through the printer, and then printing. **Note:** You can purchase pre-cut sheets of freezer paper in some quilt shops and online.

2. With the shiny side of the paper facing down and leaving at least ½" between shapes, lightly iron the templates to the RIGHT SIDE of your fabric.

3. Using a fabric marking tool, draw around the shapes. Remove shapes and reuse if needed for the required number of shapes needed. Repeat for each fabric that uses that shape.

4. Repeat Step 3 to draw all of the appliqué shapes called for in the project instructions onto your fabrics.

5. Leaving about ¼" for a seam allowance, cut out the shapes.

Paper Patterns

1. Photocopy patterns. Cut out the patterns and they become your templates. Cut ONE template for each different appliqué shape in your project instructions.

2. Place template, printed side up, on the RIGHT SIDE of your fabric. Using a fabric marking tool, draw around the shape (**Fig. 5**). Leaving at least ½" between shapes, draw the number of shapes called for in the instructions. Repeat for each fabric that uses that shape.

Fig. 5

3. Repeat Step 2 to draw all of the appliqué shapes called for in the project instructions.

4. Leaving about ¼" for a seam allowance, cut out the shapes.

Light Box

1. Photocopy pattern. Place the pattern on a light box (it helps to tape the pattern in place).

2. Lay your fabric RIGHT SIDE up over the pattern and trace. Leaving at least ½" between shapes, trace the number of shapes called for in the instructions. Repeat for each fabric and shape to draw all of the appliqué shapes called for in the project instructions..

3. Leaving about ¼" seam allowance, cut out the shapes.

   tip If you ever want to make templates to use for Needleturn Appliqué from patterns that are printed in reverse, like the patterns used for Mock Hand Appliqué, be sure to flip your templates over before drawing around them on your fabric.

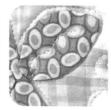

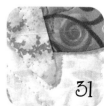

31

The Needleturn Stitch

Now is the fun part—it's you, a needle, and some thread! The goal of Needleturn Appliqué is to have nice, smooth, turned under edges on your shapes and a stitch that you don't see.

Fig. 6

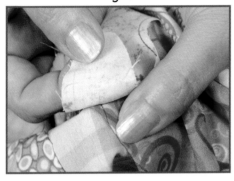

Fig. 7

Fig. 8

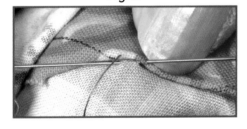

Fig. 9

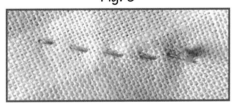

Fig. 10

 I like to work from the bottom layer up, stitching the appliqués that are closest to the background first.

1. Thread your needle with an approximately 24" length of thread and knot one end.

2. Use the tip of the needle to turn the seam allowance under for about 1" or less ahead of where you are working. For most shapes I find that I use my needle and my fingers to turn the seam allowance. I hold the folded seam allowance in place with my left thumb (**Fig. 6**).

3. Bring your needle up through the background fabric and the appliqué shape just a thread or two inside the drawn line (**Fig. 7**). The knot will be on the back of the background fabric.

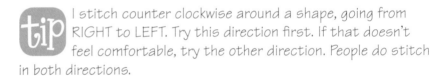 I stitch counter clockwise around a shape, going from RIGHT to LEFT. Try this direction first. If that doesn't feel comfortable, try the other direction. People do stitch in both directions.

4. I like to think of the folded edge of the shape as the "curb" and the background fabric as the "street". You want your thread to come OFF the curb and into the street in the EXACT spot where it came off the curb. Bring the needle up into the folded edge of the appliqué about ⅛" away from where the thread went into the street (**Fig. 8**).

5. Your thread "travels" on the backside of your background fabric (**Fig. 9**). Your stitches should be invisible from the right (top) side (**Fig. 10**).

6. Continue stitching around your shape. Every few stitches, tug very gently to pull the stitches FIRM. Not TIGHT, just FIRM. You don't want to ruffle your shape.

tip When a shape goes under another shape, such as a stem under a pomegranate, I only stitch the stem for about ½" UNDER the edge of the pomegranate. That's all. It's not necessary to stitch the entire part that is not seen.

7. Referring to **Pretty Points** and **Incredible Innies**, as needed, continue turning and stitching until the entire shape is stitched in place.

8. Repeat Steps 1-7 for each appliqué shape in your project.

tip I try to stitch as much as I can with the same color thread before changing to the next color. For example, I try to stitch all of the stems and leaves with the same green. Then all the red berries with the same red... etc.

Pretty Points

Fig. 11

- When approaching a point, like the tip of a leaf, turn under the entire seam allowance on the side where you are stitching. Stop stitching about 2 stitches from the point (**Fig. 11**).

- Fold the point of the seam allowance perpendicular to the point of the shape (**Fig. 12**).

   If the seam allowance is creating a lot of bulk under the point, you can peek underneath and trim some of it away.

Fig. 12

- Fold under the second side, forming a nice point.

- Finish stitching the first side and then take a stitch right in the point. Continue stitching around the shape.

Incredible Innies

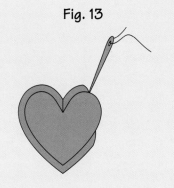

Fig. 13

- If your shape has an inward "V", at the point of the V clip the seam allowance right up to and JUST through the drawn line (**Fig. 13**).

- When you are a few stitches from the bottom of the V, use the tip of your needle to "sweep" under the seam allowances on BOTH sides of the V. Hold the turned under seam allowances down with your thumb as you stitch it in place.

   The steeper the V, the less seam allowance there is to turn under as you reach the point. Do not over work the point of the V trying to turn it under.

   Sweeping under the 2 sides of the seam allowance with a toothpick or pin dipped in basting glue will help hold the seam allowances under while you stitch.

- Stitch around the V taking several small stitches right at the point of the V.

   You may not want to heavily use or wash quilts that have lots of small appliqués with inside V's. Because there is not much seam allowance, they may fray at the points of the V's.

Pomegranate Crossing

The pomegranate, a native of the Mediterranean region, is one of the oldest fruits known to man. It is considered by many cultures to be a symbol of health, fertility, and eternal life. With its rich red skin and crown-shaped calyx, the pomegranate's easily recognizable image has been used for centuries to adorn fabric, books, buildings, and QUILTS!

When designing this quilt, I was inspired by the many antique quilts and hooked rugs that feature the pomegranate. My version uses big, whimsical appliqués in a traditional setting.

Finished Quilt Size: 59" x 59" (150 cm x 150 cm)
Finished Block Size: 20" x 20" (51 cm x 51 cm)
Machine Quilted by Cathy Leitner

FABRIC REQUIREMENTS

*Yardage is based on 43"/44" (109 cm/112 cm) wide fabric. Refer to **Selecting Fabric**, page 6, for my tips on choosing fabrics for your appliqués.*

- 1 yd (91 cm) **each** of 2 cream prints
- 1 yd (91 cm) of red print No. 1 (includes binding)
- ¼ yd (23 cm) of red print No. 2
- 14" x 11" (36 cm x 28 cm) rectangle of red print No. 3
- ¼ yd (23 cm) of red stripe
- ⅝ yd (57 cm) of gold print
- 1⅞ yds (1.7 m) of green print No. 1
- ¾ yd (69 cm) of green print No. 2
- 12" x 9" (30 cm x 23 cm) rectangle of green print No. 3
- ⅛ yd (11 cm) of purple print
- 3¾ yds (3.4 m) of backing fabric

You will also need:

- 67" x 67" (170 cm x 170 cm) square of batting
- ½" (12 mm) wide bias tape maker
- See **Supplies**, page 28, for my list of special Needleturn supplies

CUTTING THE BACKGROUND AND BORDERS

*Follow **Rotary Cutting**, page 103, to cut fabric. Cut all strips from the selvage-to-selvage width of the fabric. All measurements include ¼" seam allowances.*

From each cream print:

- Cut 8 **squares** 10½" x 10½".

From red print No. 1:

- Cut 5 strips 3" wide. From these strips, cut 60 **large squares** 3" x 3".
- Cut 1 strip 2½" wide. From this strip, cut 9 **small squares** 2½" x 2½".
- Cut 7 **binding strips** 1½"w.

From gold print:

- Cut 5 strips 3" wide. From these strips, cut 60 **large squares** 3" x 3".

From green print No. 1:

- Cut 2 lengthwise **side outer borders** 6½" x 58½".
- Cut 2 lengthwise **top/bottom outer borders** 6½" x 46½".

CUTTING THE APPLIQUÉS

*Follow **Making and Using Templates**, page 30, to cut and prepare appliqués using patterns, pages 39-41. Refer to **Making Bias Tape**, page 8, to make bias tape.*

From red print No. 1:
- Cut 8 **large circles**.

From red print No. 2:
- Cut 4 **pomegranates**.

From red print No. 3:
- Cut 4 **pomegranate crowns**.

From red stripe:
- Cut 4 **pomegranate centers**.

From gold print:
- Cut 8 **small circles**.

From green print No. 2:
- Cut 4 **large leaves**.
- Make 112" of 1/2" wide **bias tape** (finished width).

From green print No. 3:
- Cut 8 **small leaves**.

From purple print:
- Cut 12 **small circles**.

ASSEMBLING THE BLOCK BACKGROUNDS

*Follow **Piecing**, page 103, and **Pressing**, page 104, to assemble the block backgrounds. Use 1/4" seam allowances throughout.*

1. Sew 4 **cream squares** together to make **block background**. Make 4 block backgrounds.

Block Background (make 4)

ADDING THE APPLIQUÉS

*Refer to **Appliqué Basics**, page 6, to prepare your project for stitching. Follow **The Needleturn Stitch**, page 32, for technique.*

1. Cut **bias tape** into 4 **short stems**, each 13" long and 4 **long stems**, each 15" long.
2. Appliqué 1 **short stem**, 1 **long stem**, 1 **large leaf**, and 2 **small leaves** to a block background.
3. Appliqué, **pomegranate crown**, **pomegranate**, **pomegranate center**, and 3 purple **small circles** to block background.
4. Appliqué 2 **large circles** and 2 gold **small circles** to block background.
5. Repeat Steps 2-4 to make 4 **Pomegranate Blocks**.

Pomegranate Block (make 4)

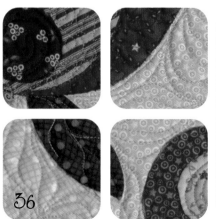

ASSEMBLING THE QUILT TOP

*Refer to photo, page 38, for placement.
Use 1/4" seam allowances throughout.*

TRIANGLE-SQUARES

I over-cut my squares when making Triangle-Squares and then trim them to the correct finished size after sewing. This insures that my Triangle-Squares will always be exactly the right size. The cutting size given in the project instructions makes Triangle-Squares that are larger than needed and the instructions tell you the size to trim the Triangle-Squares.

1. Draw a diagonal line on wrong side of each gold print **large square**. With right sides together, place 1 marked square on top of 1 red print No. 1 **large square**; pin if desired. Stitch seam 1/4" from each side of drawn line (**Fig. 1**).

Fig. 1

2. Cut along drawn line. Open and press seam allowances toward darker fabric to make 2 **Triangle-Squares**. Make 120 Triangle-Squares; trim to 2 1/2" x 2 1/2".

Triangle-Square (make 120)

SASHINGS

1. Sew 10 **Triangle-Squares** together to make 1 **short sashing strip**. Make 12 short sashing strips.

Short Sashing Strip (make 12)

2. Sew 3 short sashing strips and 2 Pomegranate blocks together to make a **row**. Make 2 rows.

Row (make 2)

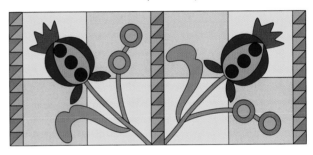

3. Sew 3 **small squares** and 2 short sashing strips together to make a **sashing row**. Make 3 sashing rows.

Sashing Row (make 3)

QUILT TOP

1. Sew rows and sashing rows together to make **quilt top center**.
2. Sew **top/bottom** and then **side outer borders** to quilt top center to make **quilt top**.

FINISHING THE QUILT

1. Follow **Quilting**, page 106, to mark, layer, and quilt. My quilt is outline quilted around the appliqués. There are detail lines quilted on each appliqué. The block backgrounds are quilted with a closely spaced echoing leaf pattern. There is a feather pattern in the outer border and a leaf and vine pattern in the inner border.

2. Refer to **Making a Hanging Sleeve**, page 109, to make and attach a hanging sleeve, if desired.

3. Use **binding strips** and follow **Pat's Machine-Sewn Binding**, page 110, to bind quilt.

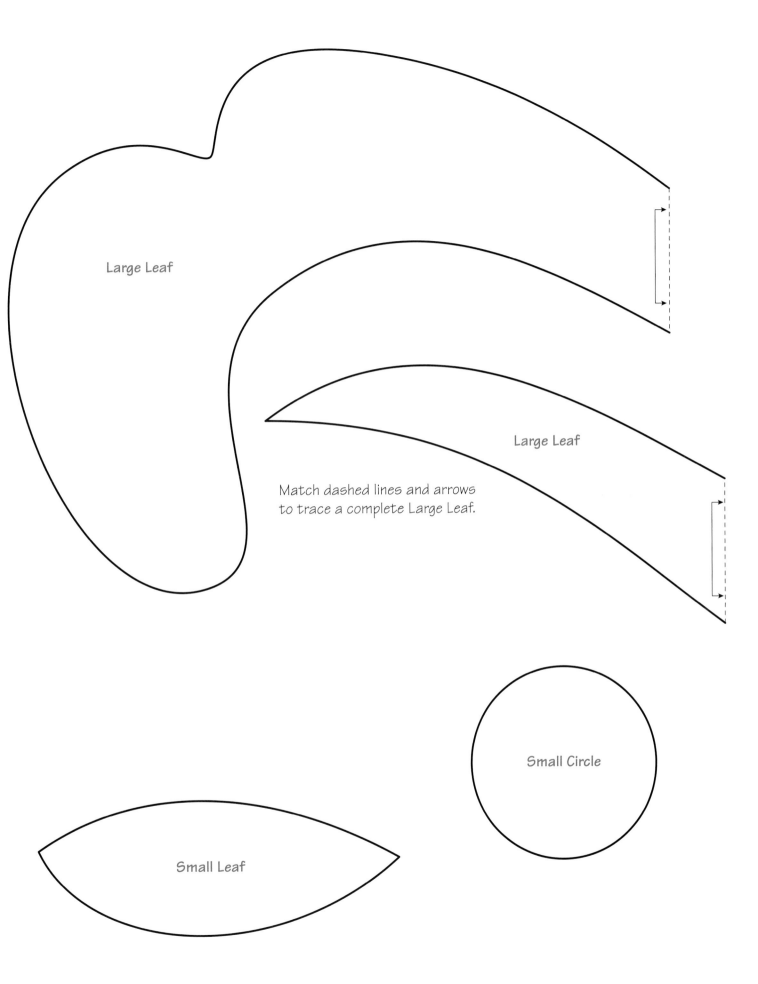

Large Leaf

Large Leaf

Match dashed lines and arrows
to trace a complete Large Leaf.

Small Circle

Small Leaf

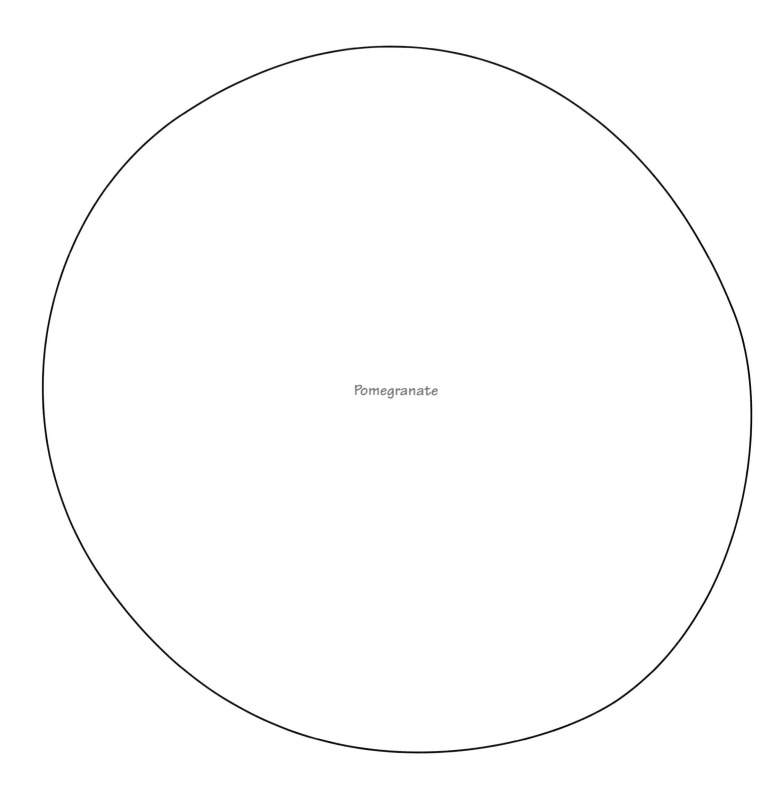

Pomegranate

40

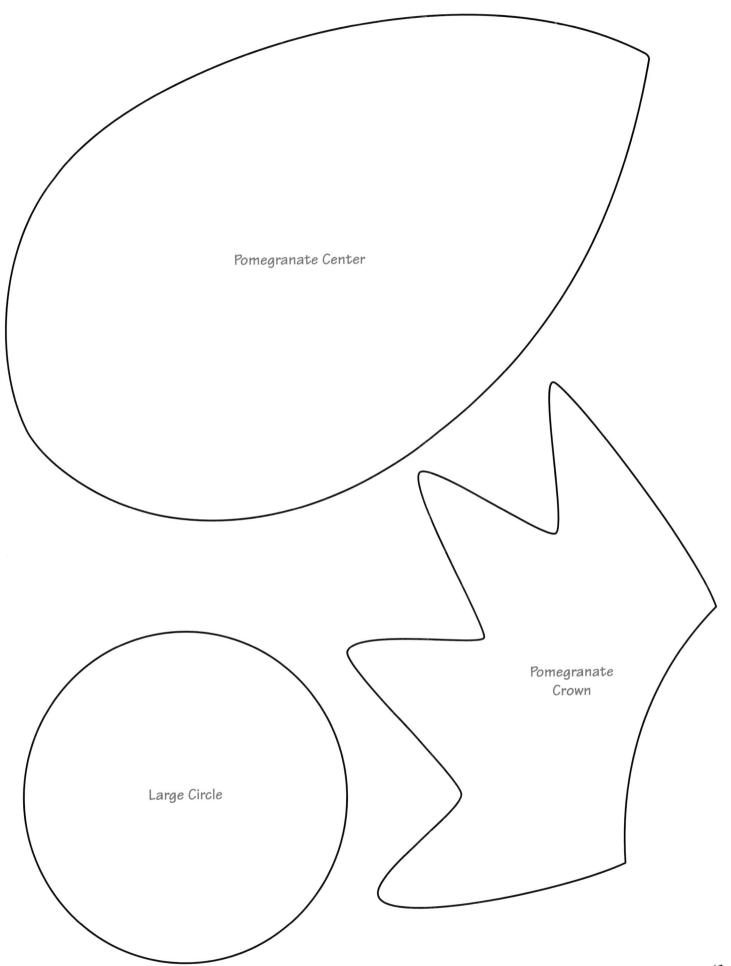

Pomegranate Center

Pomegranate
Crown

Large Circle

41

Fresh for the Picking

This fun little quilt is the perfect beginner project for learning Needleturn Appliqué! For my quilt, I chose shades of raspberry pink for a summertime look but I can also see this quilt made with deep red strawberries and a great red print border... yum, yum! Makes me want a slice of strawberry pie or bowl of strawberry ice cream!

Finished Quilt Size: 29" x 29" (74 cm x 74 cm)
Machine Quilted by Cathy Leitner

FABRIC REQUIREMENTS

Yardage is based on 43"/44" (109 cm/112 cm) wide fabric.
*Refer to **Selecting Fabric**, page 6, for my tips on choosing fabrics for your appliqués.*

- 1 fat quarter* **each** of 2 cream prints
- 1/4 yd (23 cm) of multi-color stripe
- 5/8 yd (57 cm) of raspberry floral
- 6" x 17" (15 cm x 43 cm) rectangle of raspberry print No. 1
- 3/8 yd (34 cm) of raspberry print No. 2 (includes binding)
- 1/2 yd (46 cm) of green print No. 1
- 6" x 12" (15 cm x 30 cm) rectangle **each** of green prints No. 2 and No. 3
- 1 yd (91 cm) of backing fabric

You will also need:

- 33" x 33" (84 cm x 84 cm) square of batting
- 1/2" (12 mm) wide bias tape maker
- Chalk Pencil
- See **Supplies**, page 28, for my list of special Needleturn supplies

*Fat quarter = approximately 18" x 22" (46 cm x 56 cm)

CUTTING THE BACKGROUND AND BORDERS

*Follow **Rotary Cutting**, page 103, to cut fabric. Cut all strips from the selvage-to-selvage width of the fabric. All measurements include 1/4" seam allowances.*

From each cream print:
- Cut 2 **squares** 9 1/2" x 9 1/2".

From multi-color stripe:
- Cut 2 **side inner borders** 1 1/2" x 18 1/2".
- Cut 2 **top/bottom inner borders** 1 1/2" x 20 1/2".

From raspberry floral:
- Cut 2 **side outer borders** 4 1/2" x 20 1/2".
- Cut 2 **top/bottom outer borders** 4 1/2" x 28 1/2".

From raspberry print No. 2:
- Cut 4 **binding strips** 1 1/2"w.

CUTTING THE APPLIQUÉS

Follow **Making and Using Templates**, page 30, to cut and prepare appliqués using patterns, pages 45-46. Refer to **Making Bias Tape**, page 8, to make bias tape,

From raspberry print No. 1:
- Cut 3 **strawberries**.

From raspberry print No. 2:
- Cut 3 **strawberries**.

From green print No. 1:
- Cut 12 **leaves**.
- Make 32" of ½" wide bias tape (finished width).

From *each* green print No. 2 and No. 3:
- Cut 3 **stems**.
- Cut 3 **strawberry caps**.

ASSEMBLING THE QUILT TOP

Follow **Piecing**, page 103, and **Pressing**, page 104, to assemble the quilt top. Use ¼" seam allowances throughout.
1. Sew 4 **cream squares** together to make **quilt top center**.
2. Sew **side** and then **top/bottom inner borders** to quilt top center.
3. Sew **side** and then **top/bottom outer borders** to quilt top center to make **quilt top**.

ADDING THE APPLIQUÉS

Refer to **Appliqué Basics**, page 6, to prepare your project for stitching. Follow **The Needleturn Stitch**, page 32, for technique.
1. Photocopy or trace the placement guide, page 46; cut out. Position guide on background and lightly draw around it with a chalk pencil.
2. Using drawn circle as a guide, arrange bias tape on quilt top, making sure raw ends will be covered by leaves. Appliqué **bias tape** in a circle to quilt top.
3. Appliqué 6 **strawberries**, 6 **strawberry caps**, and 6 **stems** to quilt top.
4. Appliqué 12 **leaves** to quilt top.

FINISHING THE QUILT

1. Follow **Quilting**, page 106, to mark, layer, and quilt. My quilt is quilted with outline quilting around the appliqués. There are detail lines quilted on each appliqué. There is a leaf and vine pattern in the background and outer border. There is a wavy line in the inner border.
2. Refer to **Making a Hanging Sleeve**, page 109, to make and attach a hanging sleeve, if desired.
3. Use **binding strips** and follow **Pat's Machine-Sewn Binding**, page 110, to bind quilt.

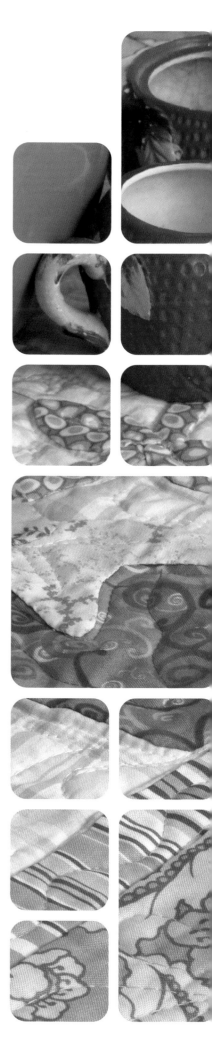

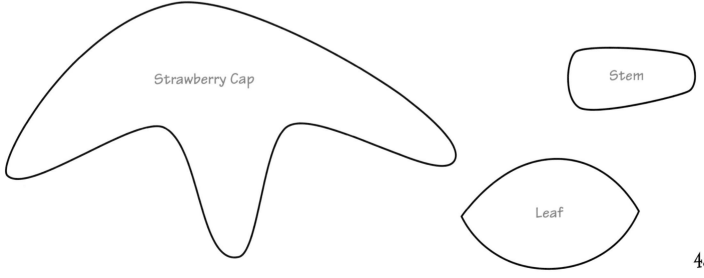

Strawberry Cap

Stem

Leaf

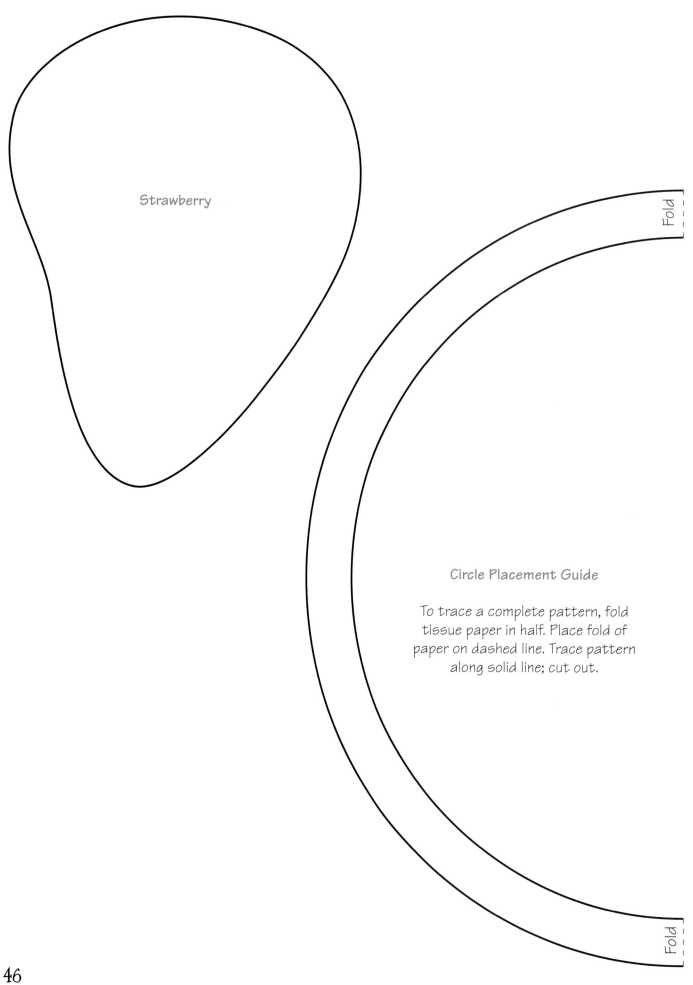

Strawberry

Circle Placement Guide

To trace a complete pattern, fold
tissue paper in half. Place fold of
paper on dashed line. Trace pattern
along solid line; cut out.

Fold

Fold

Running Stitch Appliqué

Running Stitch appliqué is very similar to Needleturn appliqué.
I make my templates and prepare my appliqués exactly the same,
but to me the stitching is faster and easier.

I first heard of this method years ago on an Internet quilt history site.
Someone was telling the story of finding what looked like "basting" stitches on
the edges of appliqués. When they picked at the basting, they discovered it was
actually the appliqué stitches. I thought this was a fabulous method of appliqué!

I find this to be an excellent technique for people who find Needleturn hard
on their eyes, who might have limitations with their hands, or for those
who just want to hand appliqué faster!

Supplies

I use the same supplies listed in **Needleturn Appliqué**, page 28, with the exception of the *thread*. With
Running Stitch Appliqué, you want your stitches to show. I like to use a contrasting thread color or even a
heavier weight than the 60-weight matching thread I use for Needleturn.

The Running Stitch

Like Needleturn, the goal of Running Stitch is to have nice, smooth, turned under edges on your shapes. Unlike Needleturn, you don't have to worry about hiding your stitches. There they are — right on top! This is very freeing to me!

Fig. 1

Fig. 2

Fig. 3

Fig. 4

 I like to work from the bottom layer up, stitching the appliqués that are closest to the background first.

1. Thread your needle with an approximately 24" length of thread and knot one end.
2. Use the tip of the needle to turn the seam allowance under for about 1" ahead of where you are working (**Fig. 1**); less for small pieces and near curves. For most shapes I find that I use my needle and my fingers to turn the seam allowance. I hold the folded seam allowance in place with my left thumb (**Fig. 2**).
3. Bring your needle up through the background and appliqué about 1/8" inside the drawn line (**Fig. 3**). The knot will be on the back of the background fabric.

 I stitch counter clockwise around a shape, going from RIGHT to LEFT. Try this direction first. If that doesn't feel comfortable, try the other direction. People do stitch in both directions.

4. Take the needle down through the appliqué and background making a stitch about 1/8"-1/4" long. "Rock" the needle through the layers to load 3 stitches onto the needle in one continuous motion. (**Fig. 4**). Firmly pull the stitches through the appliqué.

 While smaller stitches are pretty, small stitches are not as important as consistent stitch length.

5. Continue stitching around your shape. Every few stitches, tug very gently to pull the stitches FIRM. Not TIGHT, just FIRM. You don't want to ruffle your shape. This is not as critical as when doing Needleturn. Most people seem to pull firmly enough when they pull the stitches through the first time.

 For better control in tight areas and around curves, I "stab stitch" one stitch at a time rather than "rocking" several stitches onto the needle.

 I do find that sometimes I need to revert to Needleturn when stitching very small shapes. Since the Running Stitch is a longer stitch it doesn't always work well for small shapes.

 When a shape goes under another shape, such as a stem under a leaf, I only stitch the stem for about ½" UNDER the edge of the leaf. That's all. It's not necessary to stitch the entire part that is not seen.

6. Referring to **Pretty Points** and **Incredible Innies**, page 33, as needed, continue turning and stitching until the entire shape is stitched in place.
7. Repeat Steps 1-6 for each appliqué shape in your project.

 I try to stitch as much as I can with the same color thread before changing to the next color. For example, I try to stitch all of the stems and leaves with the same green. Then all the red berries with the same red... etc.

Quilters in Paradise

Have you ever been on a quilting cruise? What a FUN getaway for you and your quilting friends! You can even take your spouse or a non-quilting girlfriend — cruise ships have loads of activities for everyone!

I designed this quilt to celebrate Quilters In Paradise, a winter getaway to the Caribbean that takes place about the time that we have three feet of snow at home! I chose Running Stitch Appliqué for this project because I think it is a fabulous appliqué technique! It's fun, easy, and relaxing — everything a vacation should be!

To join me on a trip to Paradise, check the workshop schedule on my website for the dates for my next cruise.

Finished Quilt Size: 42" x 48" (107 cm x 122 cm)

FABRIC REQUIREMENTS

Refer to **Selecting Fabric**, page 6, for my tips on choosing fabrics for your appliqués. Yardage is based on 43"/44" (109 cm/112 cm) wide fabric.

- 1 yd (91 cm) of white print
- 1 yd (91 cm) of multi-color batik (includes binding)
- ³/₈ yd (34 cm) of pink batik
- ⁵/₈ yd (57 cm) **total** of assorted blue, purple, and green batiks
- Fat quarters* or large scraps of assorted batiks for appliqués; pink, tan, purple, blue, green, yellow, and orange
- 3 yds (2.7 m)) of backing fabric

You will also need:
- 46" x 52" (117 cm x 132 cm) rectangle of batting
- Template plastic, paper, or freezer paper

*Fat quarter = approximately 18" x 22" (46 cm x 56 cm)

CUTTING THE BACKGROUND AND BORDERS

Follow **Rotary Cutting**, page 103, to cut fabric. Cut all strips from the selvage-to-selvage width of the fabric. All measurements include ¹/₄" seam allowances.

From white print:
- Cut 1 strip 12¹/₂" wide. From this strip, cut 1 **rectangle** 12¹/₂" x 14¹/₂" (**B**) and 1 **rectangle** 16¹/₂" x 12¹/₂" (**E**).
- Cut 1 strip 8¹/₂" wide. From this strip, cut 1 **rectangle** 8¹/₂" x 16¹/₂" (**C**) and 1 **rectangle** 8¹/₂" x 22¹/₂" (**D**).
- Cut 1 **rectangle** 24¹/₂" x 8¹/₂" (**A**).

From multi-color batik:
- Cut 2 **top/bottom outer borders** 4¹/₂" x 33¹/₂".
- Cut 2 **side outer borders** 4¹/₂" x 39¹/₂".
- Cut 5 **binding strips** 1¹/₂" wide.

From pink batik:
- Cut 2 **top/bottom inner borders** 1" x 33¹/₂".
- Cut 2 **side inner borders** 1" x 38¹/₂".
- Cut 4 **corner squares** 4¹/₂" x 4¹/₂".

From assorted blue, purple, and green batiks:
- Cut 23 **smallest rectangles** 2¹/₂" x 4¹/₂" (**F**).
- Cut 1 **small rectangle** 8¹/₂" x 2¹/₂" (**G**).
- Cut 2 **medium rectangles** 2¹/₂" x 12¹/₂" (**H**).
- Cut 1 **large rectangle** 4¹/₂" x 12¹/₂" (**I**).
- Cut 2 **largest rectangles** 16¹/₂" x 2¹/₂" (**J**).

CUTTING THE APPLIQUÉS

*Follow **Making and Using Templates**, page 30, to cut and prepare appliqués using patterns, pages 56-61.*

From multi-color batik:
- Cut 6 scallop bubbles.

From assorted pink batiks:
- Cut 1 small star.
- Cut 1 heart.
- Cut 1 of *each* hibiscus petal 1-5.
- Cut 1 hibiscus bud.
- Cut 3 seahorse mane rectangles.
- Cut 1 seahorse back fin.
- Cut 1 leaf accent. Cut 1 leaf accent reversed.

From tan batik:
- Cut 1 mermaid head/right arm.
- Cut 1 mermaid left arm.

From assorted purple batiks:
- Cut 1 hibiscus center.
- Cut 5 scallop accents.

From assorted blue batiks:
- Cut 1 mermaid body.
- Cut 3 seahorse bubbles.
- Cut 4 stamens.
- Cut 1 scallop base.

From assorted green batiks:
- Cut 2 hibiscus leaves.
- Cut 1 hibiscus stem.
- Cut 1 hibiscus calyx.
- Cut 1 hibiscus stamen.
- Cut 1 seahorse side fin.
- Cut 1 seahorse body.
- Cut 1 large leaf. Cut 1 large leaf reversed.
- Cut 1 small leaf. Cut 1 small leaf reversed.

From assorted yellow batiks:
- Cut 7 small stars.
- Cut 4 large stars.
- Cut 1 of *each* mermaid hair section 1-3.
- Cut 1 seahorse eye.

From assorted orange batiks:
- Cut 1 scallop shell.
- Cut 1 scallop foot. Cut 1 scallop foot reversed.
- Cut 1 large flower. Cut 1 large flower reversed.
- Cut 1 small flower. Cut 1 small flower reversed.

ASSEMBLING THE QUILT TOP

*Follow **Piecing**, page 103, and **Pressing**, page 104, to assemble the quilt top. Refer to **Assembly Diagram**, page 55, for placement. Use ¼" seam allowances throughout.*

1. Sew 4 **smallest rectangles (F)** together to make **Unit 1**. Repeat to make 2 **Unit 1's**.

Unit 1 (make 2)

2. Sew 1 **Unit 1** to each short end of **rectangle A** to make **Unit 2**.

Unit 2

3. Sew 2 **largest rectangles (J)** together to make **Unit 3**.

Unit 3

4. Sew **Units 2** and **3** together to make **Unit 4**.

Unit 4

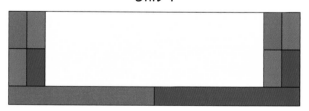

5. Sew 5 **smallest rectangles (F)** together to make **Unit 5**.

Unit 5

6. Sew 6 **smallest rectangles** (F) together to make Unit 6.

Unit 6

7. Sew **small rectangle** (G) to one short edge of rectangle D to make **Unit 7**.

Unit 7

8. Sew **Units 5, 6,** and **7** together to make **Unit 8**.

Unit 8

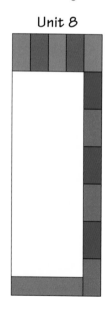

9. Sew 4 **smallest rectangles** (F) together to make Unit 9.

Unit 9

10. Sew 1 **medium rectangle** (H) to one short edge of **rectangle B** to make **Unit 10**.

Unit 10

11. Sew **Units 9, 10,** and **rectangle C** together to make **Unit 11**.

Unit 11

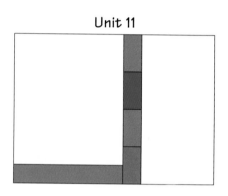

12. Sew 1 **medium rectangle** (H) and **large rectangle** (I) to short sides of **rectangle E** to make **Unit 12**.

Unit 12

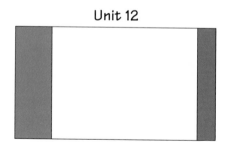

13. Sew **Units 4, 8, 11,** and **12** together to make **quilt top center**.
14. Sew **side** and then **top/bottom inner borders** to quilt top center.
15. Sew 1 **corner square** to each end of top/bottom outer borders.
16. Sew **side** and then **top/bottom outer borders** to quilt top center to make **quilt top**.

ADDING THE APPLIQUÉS

*Refer to **Appliqué Basics**, page 6, to prepare your project for stitching. Follow **The Running Stitch**, page 48, for technique.*

Mermaid

1. Appliqué **mermaid left arm** and **head/right arm** to quilt top.
2. Appliqué **mermaid body**, 3 **mermaid hair sections**, **heart**, and pink **small star** to quilt top.
3. Appliqué 3 yellow **small stars** and 1 yellow **large star** to quilt top.

Bird of Paradise

1. Appliqué the *lower* **large leaf, stamens, large flower, small flower,** pink **leaf accent,** and **small leaf.**
2. Appliqué the *upper* **large leaf reversed, stamens reversed, large flower reversed, small flower reversed,** pink **leaf accent reversed,** and **small leaf reversed.**
3. Appliqué 2 yellow **small stars** and 1 yellow **large star** to quilt top.

Hibiscus

1. Appliqué **hibiscus stem,** 2 **hibiscus leaves, hibiscus bud,** and **hibiscus calyx** to the quilt top.
2. Appliqué **hibiscus center,** 5 **hibiscus petals,** and **hibiscus stamen** to the quilt top.

Seahorse

1. Appliqué **seahorse back fin, seahorse body,** 3 **seahorse mane rectangles, seahorse eye,** and **seahorse side fin** to the quilt top.
2. Appliqué 3 **seahorse bubbles** to the quilt top.

Scallop

1. Appliqué **scallop foot, scallop foot reversed,** and **scallop shell,** to the quilt top.
2. Appliqué **scallop accents** and **scallop base** to the quilt top.
3. Appliqué **scallop bubbles,** 2 yellow **small stars** and 2 **large stars** to the quilt top.

FINISHING THE QUILT

1. Follow **Quilting**, page 106, to mark, layer, and quilt. My quilt is quilted with outline quilting around the appliqués and detail lines on the appliqués. There are bubbles in the block backgrounds and waves in the blue sashings. There is a wide wave that follows the print of the fabric in the outer border.
2. Refer to **Making a Hanging Sleeve**, page 109, to make and attach a hanging sleeve, if desired.
3. Use **binding strips** and follow **Pat's Machine-Sewn Binding**, page 110, to bind quilt.

Assembly Diagram

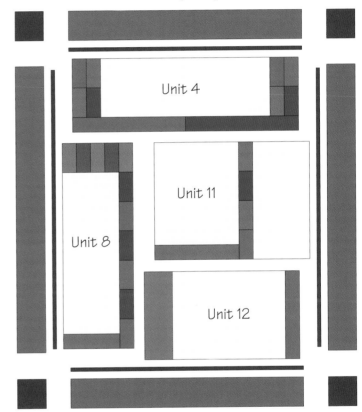

55

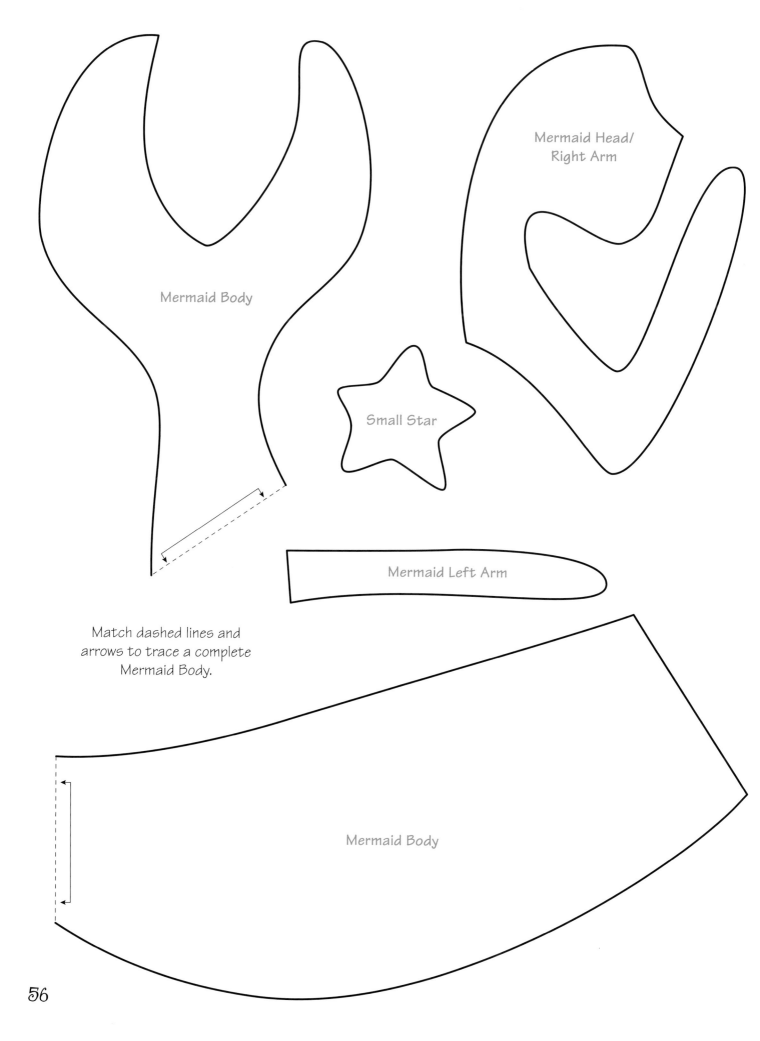

Mermaid Body

Mermaid Head/
Right Arm

Small Star

Mermaid Left Arm

Match dashed lines and
arrows to trace a complete
Mermaid Body.

Mermaid Body

56

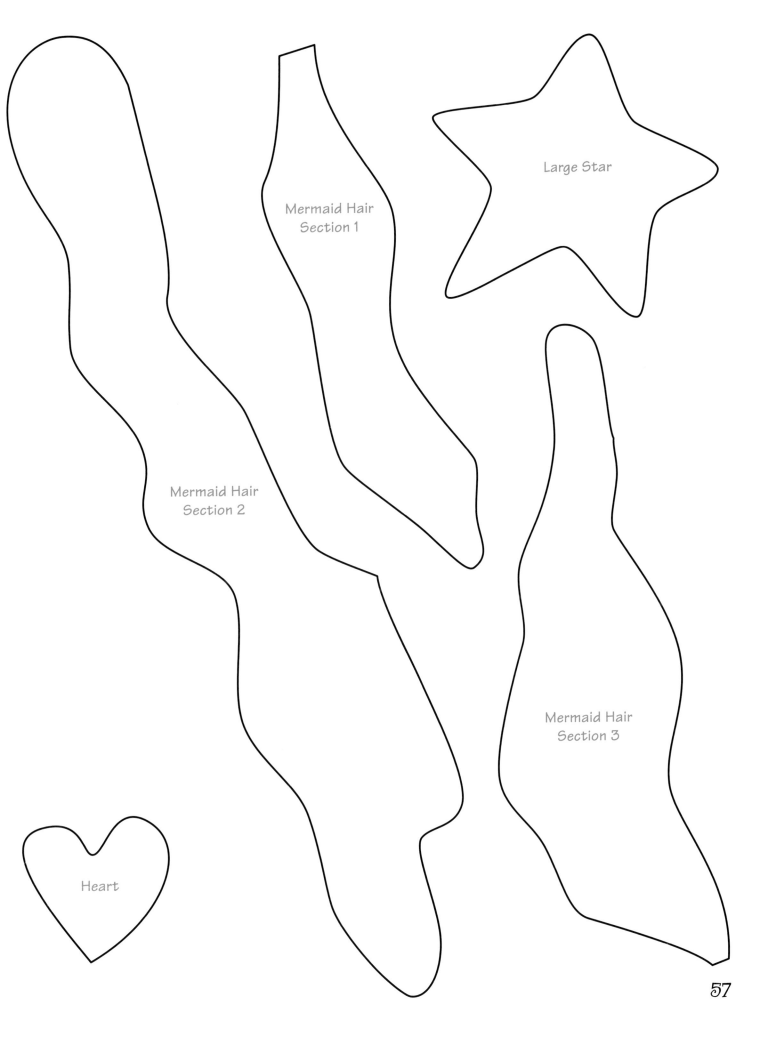

Mermaid Hair
Section 1

Large Star

Mermaid Hair
Section 2

Mermaid Hair
Section 3

Heart

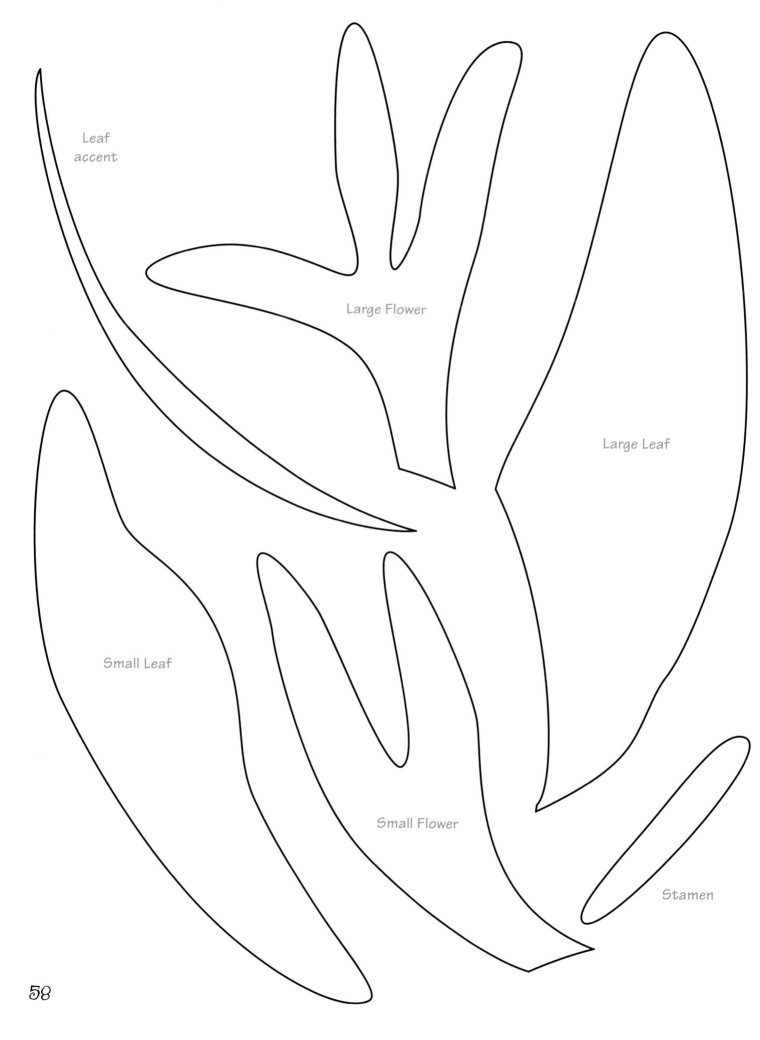

Leaf
accent

Large Flower

Large Leaf

Small Leaf

Small Flower

Stamen

58

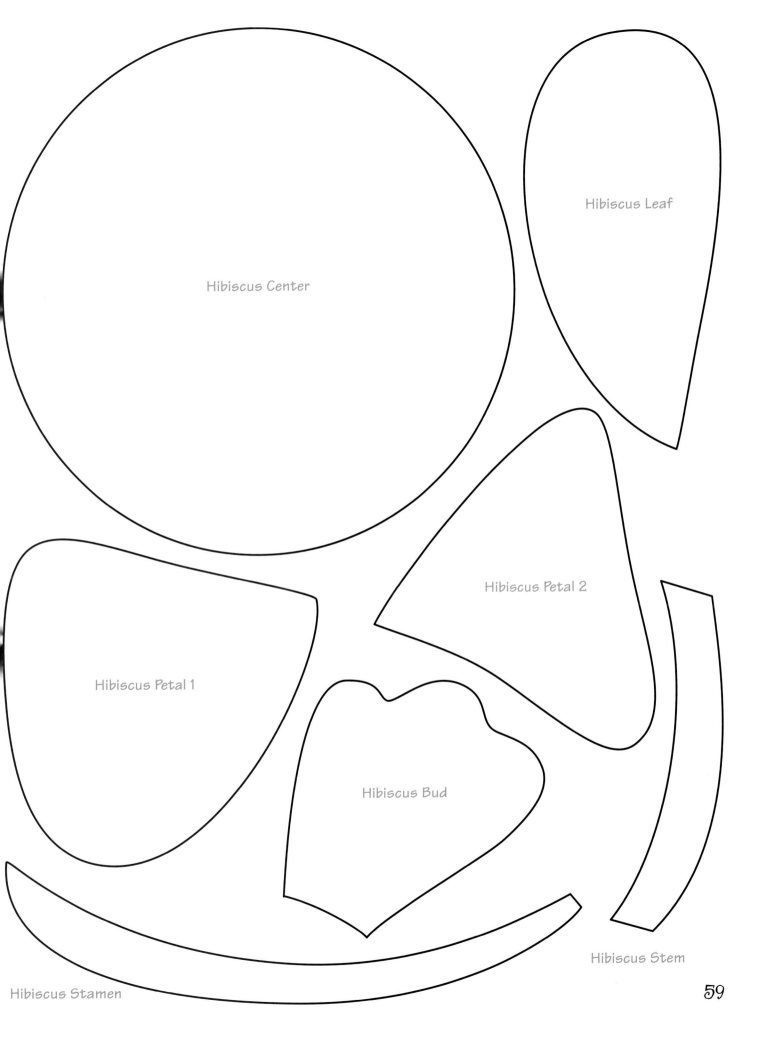

Hibiscus Center

Hibiscus Leaf

Hibiscus Petal 2

Hibiscus Petal 1

Hibiscus Bud

Hibiscus Stem

Hibiscus Stamen

59

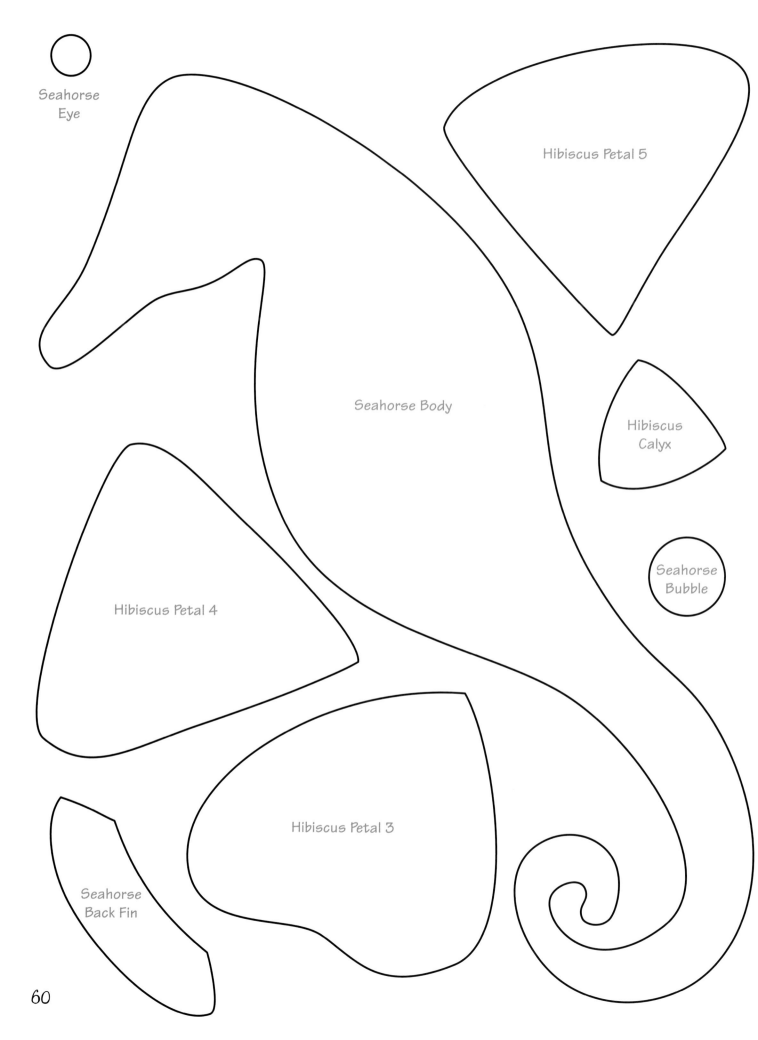

Seahorse
Eye

Hibiscus Petal 5

Seahorse Body

Hibiscus
Calyx

Hibiscus Petal 4

Seahorse
Bubble

Hibiscus Petal 3

Seahorse
Back Fin

60

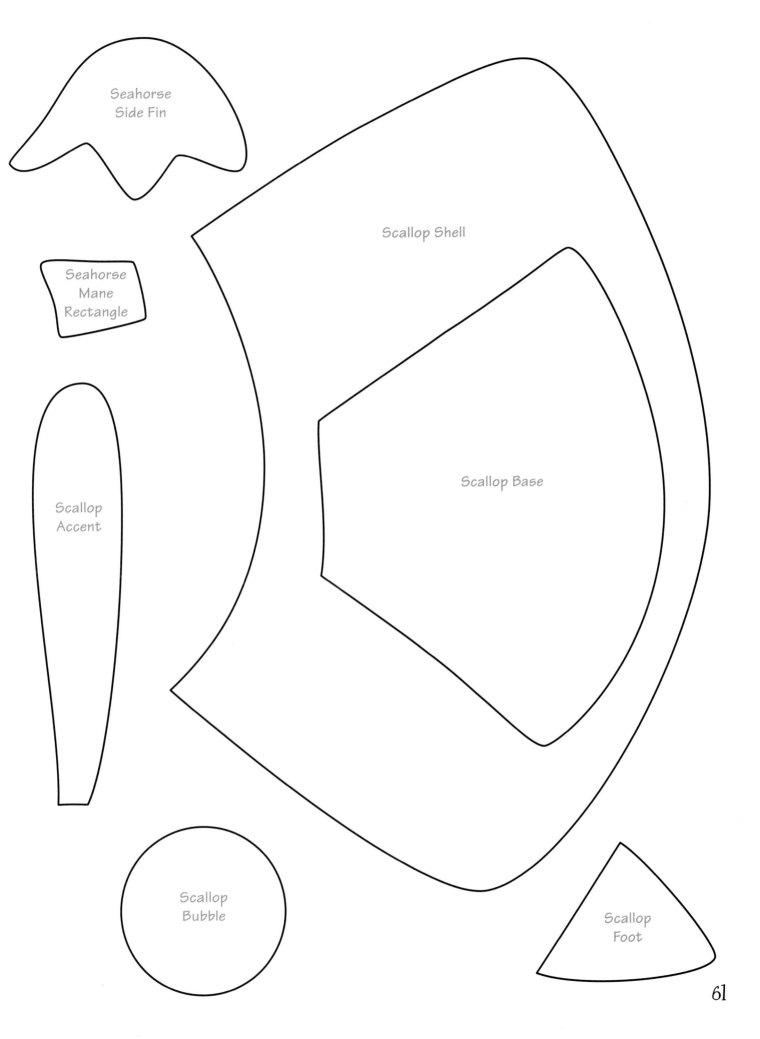

Seahorse Side Fin

Seahorse Mane Rectangle

Scallop Shell

Scallop Accent

Scallop Base

Scallop Bubble

Scallop Foot

61

Seashell Tote

For your future cruise (or even just a quick trip to the lake), whip up this handy tote! I used the scallop appliqué design from the Quilters in Paradise quilt to add a bit of fun.

Finished Tote Size: 18" x 18" (46 cm x 46 cm)

FABRIC REQUIREMENTS

Refer to **Selecting Fabrics**, page 6, for my tips on choosing fabrics for your appliqués. Yardage is based on 43"/44" (109 cm/112 cm) wide fabric.

- $^3/_8$ yd (34 cm) of green print
- $^1/_2$ yd (46 cm) of novelty print
- Scraps of teal, maroon, and purple prints

You will also need:

- 2 squares 18" x 18" (46 cm x 46 cm) of white vinyl mesh (available at fabric and craft stores)
- 16" x 38" (41 cm x 97 cm) rectangle of batting
- Template plastic, paper, or freezer paper

Working with Webbing
- *Use lots of pins to keep fabric from shifting on the webbing.*
- *Use your walking foot.*
- *Change the needle when you're done!*

CUTTING OUT THE PIECES

Follow **Rotary Cutting**, page 103, to cut fabric. Cut all strips from the selvage-to-selvage width of the fabric. All measurements include $^1/_4$" seam allowances.

From green print:
- Cut 2 **rectangles** 18" x 11".

From novelty print:
- Cut 2 **handle strips** $3^1/_4$" x 70", pieced as necessary.
- Cut 2 **trim strips** $1^3/_4$" x 18.

From batting:
- Cut 1 **rectangle** 18" x 11".
- Cut 2 **strips** 1" x 35".
- Cut 4 **strips** 1" x $17^1/_2$".

CUTTING THE APPLIQUÉS

Follow **Making and Using Templates**, page 30, to cut and prepare appliqués using patterns, page 61.

From teal print fabric:
- Cut 1 **scallop shell**.
- Cut 1 **scallop foot**. Cut 1 **scallop foot reversed**.

From maroon print fabric:
- Cut 1 **scallop base**.

From purple print fabric:
- Cut 3 **scallop accents**.

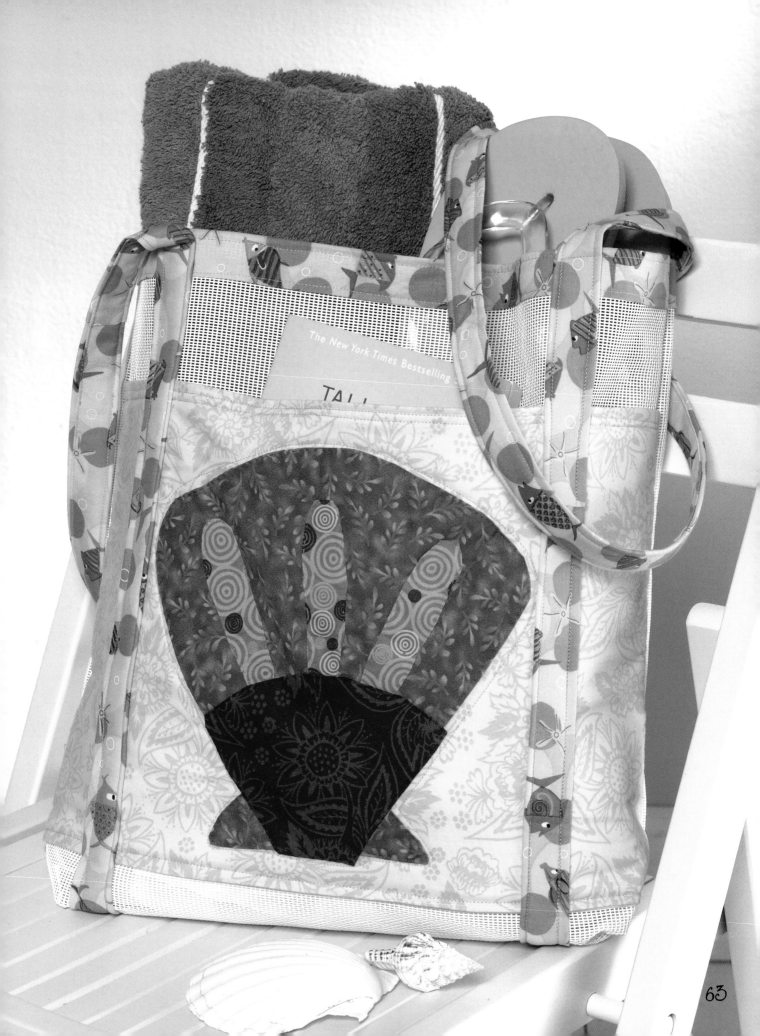

ADDING THE APPLIQUÉS

*Refer to **Appliqué Basics**, page 6, to arrange and baste your appliqués onto 1 green print rectangle. Follow **The Running Stitch**, page 48, for technique.*

1. Appliqué **scallop foot**, **scallop foot** reversed, and **scallop shell**, to the rectangle.
2. Appliqué **scallop accents** and **scallop base** to the rectangle.

ASSEMBLING THE TOTE

*Follow **Piecing**, page 103, and **Pressing**, page 104, to assemble the tote. Refer to photo, page 65, for placement. Use 1/4" seam allowances throughout.*

1. For pocket, layer remaining green **rectangle** (right side up), batting rectangle, and appliquéd rectangle (right side down). Pin layers together and stitch across top and bottom (long) edges. Turn right side out and press.
2. Topstitch a line across pocket 1/4" from top edge. Topstitch a second line 1/2" from top edge. Outline quilt (page 106) around appliqué design to complete pocket.

Pocket

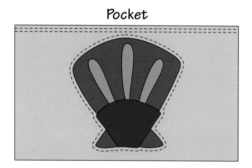

3. Position the pocket 4" from the bottom edge of 1 webbing square. Topstitch the bottom edge of the pocket to the square.
4. Press 1 long edge of 1 **trim strip** 1/4" to wrong side. With raw edges aligned and with right side of strip facing wrong side of web, sew strip to webbing. Fold strip over webbing and topstitch 1/8" from top and bottom edges of trim to complete tote front. Repeat to add trim strip to remaining webbing square for tote back.

5. Fold and press 1 long edge of 1 **handle strip** 1/2" to wrong side (**Fig. 1**).

Fig. 1

6. Center long batting strip in center of handle. Butt short ends of 2 short batting strips to either end of a long batting strip (**Fig. 2**). Press right edge of handle over batting (**Fig. 3**).

Fig. 2   Fig. 3

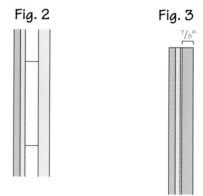

7. Press left edge over to cover raw edge and batting. Top stitch close to folded edge. Topstitch an equal distance from opposite side (**Fig. 4**). Repeat for remaining handle.

Fig. 4

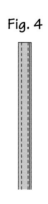

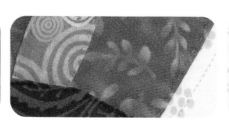

8. With 1 end of handle aligned with bottom edge, position handle on tote front 3" from left side of tote front. Position remaining end of handle 3" from right side of tote front. Topstitch handle to tote front along sides of handle and across handle ¼" from top edge of tote front (**Fig. 5**).

Fig. 5

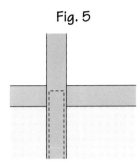

9. In the same manner, topstitch remaining handle to tote back.

10. Sew tote front and tote back together at sides and bottom edges.

11. To make boxed corners, turn tote wrong side out. Match side seam with bottom seam and sew across 1 bottom corner 3½" from tip (**Fig 6**). Trim seam allowance to ¼". Repeat for remaining bottom corner.

Fig. 6

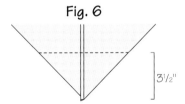

3½"

Utility Quilting

I love the look, feel, and texture of hand quilting, but traditional fine hand quilting takes so long and my wrists don't like it very much. So a few years ago I gave Utility (or big stitch, or running stitch) quilting a try. THIS I love to do! It's easier than fine hand quilting, more forgiving to my wrists, and fits my schedule better.

Supplies

In addition to my fabric and basic sewing supplies, there are a few special supplies I use when Utility Quilting.

- **Fabric Marking Tools** – There are many types of fabric marking tools available. See **Choosing The Right Fabric Marking Tool** to learn more about your choices. Whichever tool you decide to use *must be removable.* You don't want marks left on your quilt top! Be sure to read the manufacturer's instructions for removal AND do a test sample before marking your quilt top.

- **Thread** – The type of thread you select will make a big difference in the look of your finished quilt. Many people prefer a heavy thread like No. 8 pearl cotton, but I usually choose a thinner thread like sewing or hand quilting thread. See **Choosing The Right Thread**, page 68, to learn about your options.

- **Batting** – I like to use a thin batting that is easy to "needle" through — meaning that you can "rock" more than one stitch onto your needle at a time. Also, it is not hard to push the needle though the quilt sandwich. Some of my favorites include 100% cottons, such as Cream Rose by Mountain Mist®, Quilters Dream®, and Hobbs Heirloom®. I also like battings with a high silk or wool content.

tip To try a batting without cutting up your large piece, cut two 8" squares of fabric and make a quilt "sandwich" on one corner of the batting. Quilt the sandwich and then remove the stitches. Your large piece of batting can still be used in a quilt!

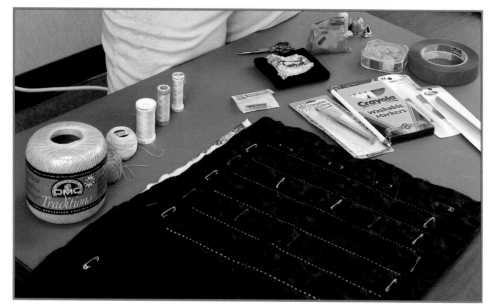

- **Needles** – For quilting with sewing or hand quilting thread I usually use a short needle, such as a Sharp, in a size 9, 10, or 11. I do like Roxanne's™ Appliqué Needles which are a hybrid (not as long as a Straw needle or as short as a Sharp). Some quilters like to use a Between — if it works for you that's great!

  For quilting with thicker threads an Embroidery size 1 - 5, Chenille size 20 - 24, or Crewel size 3 - 9 works well for most people. You don't want too large a needle or you will have trouble loading more than one stitch at a time on the needle.

- **Needle Threader** – I love my Clover Desk Needle Threader for threading small-eye needles with sewing weight threads (see **Figs. 1-2**, page 29). Unfortunately, it doesn't work with large-eye needles and thick thread. For those I have a couple of tips, page 69, that I have learned from my students, see **Threading Your Needle**.

- **Thimble** – I prefer a metal or thick leather thimble. I wear it on the middle finger of my right hand (my "pushing finger"). Because I push the needle through the fabric with the SIDE of my finger, I use a thimble with dimples on the sides. Many people push from the tip of their finger, so they would want a thimble with dimples on the top. This is a very personal choice and you may have to try several thimbles until you find the one that's best for you.

Choosing the Right Fabric Marking Tool

Tape – This is my favorite way to mark because I don't have to draw on the quilt top. There are several brands made just for quilters. Blue painter's tape also works well and is available in different widths.

White Soap Slivers – These work great! They make a thin line and are easy to remove. I first heard about using soap slivers as marking tools from a textile restorer at a Williamsburg, Virginia museum (see photo, below).

Fabric Marking Pencils – These are available in chalk and charcoal. They usually work great on dark fabrics because the marks are easy to see. One of the brands I like is General® Charcoal White®.

Water-Soluble Fabric Markers – These come in limited colors and can be hard to see on prints. Some quilters have had difficulty removing the marks from some brands that claim to wash out. Be sure to test!

Watercolor Pencils – The brand I like is Caran d'Ache® Supracolor. I only use white, gold, or silver and I draw very lightly. These can be found in art supply stores.

Choosing the Right Thread

Stitching a thread sampler, similar to the one shown below, is a great way to learn about thread. You can see which threads produce the look you want and which ones are the easiest to work with. Using 2 rectangles of scrap fabric and a piece of batting, simply make a quilt sandwich. Pin-baste the layers, draw several stitching lines, and have fun quilting!

50- or 60-Weight Sewing Thread – Because it is so thin this thread is easy to quilt with. It adds texture without being a "design feature" on a quilt. I like Mettler® Silk-Finish 100% cotton and Aurifil™ 50 Cotton Makó. The Aurifil™ is spun very thin, which I like very much.

Hand Quilting Thread – This thread is heavier than sewing thread but is still easy to pull through the quilt layers. Mettler® Hand/Machine Quilting Thread made from 100% Egyptian cotton is one of my favorites.

Embroidery Floss – Floss is readily available in loads of colors and it's fairly easy to pull through the quilt layers. I recommend separating the strands and using just 3 of the 6 strands.

Pearl Cotton No. 8, 10, or 12 – This thread is available in lots of colors, sizes, and is easy to find. The thickness of the thread decreases as the number increases. The drawback is that many people have trouble pulling it through a quilt.

Cotton Crochet Thread No. 10, 20, or 30 – Similar in size to pearl cotton but with a harder finish, this thread really stands out to make your quilting a design feature. Like pearl cotton, the thickness of the thread decreases as the number increases and it can be difficult to pull through.

tip If you like the look of thick thread, but need help pulling the needle through the quilt layers, try using a piece of rubber cut from a jar opener as a gripper.

Threading Your Needle

Here's a few tips I've learned for threading my needle with those thicker threads.

It's Magic

1. Lay the thread over the index finger of your non-sewing hand with about 3" of thread facing you and the remaining thread hanging off the opposite side of your finger (Fig. 1). Grasp thread with your thumb and middle fingers and hold firmly but not tightly. (Fig. 2).

2. Holding the needle, with your sewing hand, on top of and parallel to the thread, gently rub the eye of the needle back and forth over the thread until a tiny loop of thread pulls through the eye (Figs. 3-4).

3. Slightly release the tension on the thread to allow more of the loop to be pulled into the eye (Fig. 5). Grab the loop, pull, and your needle is threaded (Fig. 6)! **Note:** If the eye of your needle is too small for the thread it won't work.

Loop Method

1. Cut about a 4" length of sewing weight thread. Fold it in half (Fig. 7).

2. Place the fold through the eye of the needle until about 1" of the fold comes out the other side making a loop (Fig. 8).

3. Thread one end of the thick thread through the loop (Fig. 9).

4. Pull the loop BACK OUT of the eye, bringing the thick thread with it and voila — your needle is threaded (Fig. 10)!

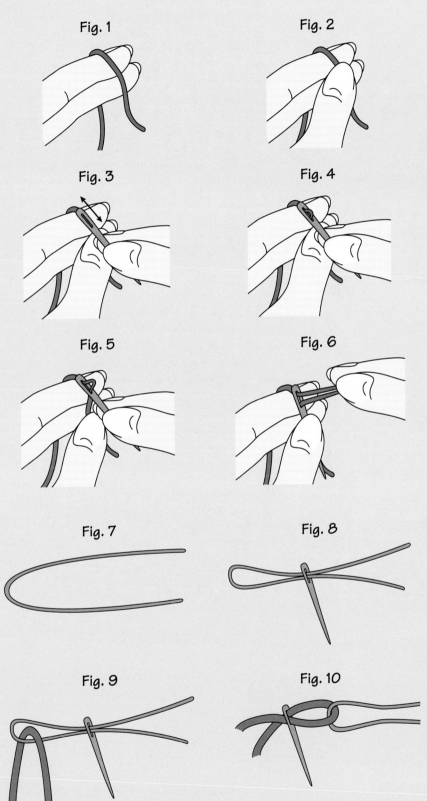

Fig. 1 Fig. 2 Fig. 3 Fig. 4 Fig. 5 Fig. 6 Fig. 7 Fig. 8 Fig. 9 Fig. 10

Preparing to Quilt

Quilting holds the three layers (top, batting, and backing) of the quilt together. Because marking and basting are interrelated and may be done in different orders depending on your preference, please read entire **Preparing To Quilt** section, pages 70 - 71, before beginning project.

BASTING

The goal of basting is to keep the layers of the quilt sandwich from shifting when quilting. Basting can be done before or after marking your quilt top. When you are ready to baste, refer to **Preparing The Backing**, page 107, to prepare your backing and **Assembling The Quilt**, page 108, to make your quilt sandwich.

MARKING THE QUILT TOP

When Utility Quilting, I usually stitch a very simple quilting design. Some of my favorites include diagonal cross-hatching, straight horizontal and vertical parallel lines, and a simple all-over design like a Baptist Fan.

Note: Utility Quilting does not have to be simple. You can use it to follow a pieced block design, make interesting quilting lines like smoke out of a chimney, or even write your name! But for this book I'm just introducing you to the technique… from here you can take it anywhere!

When To Mark

When you are ready to mark you have some decisions to make. You can mark before you layer and baste the quilt or after. There are advantages and disadvantages to both ways. I usually layer and baste first and then mark a section at a time, right before I quilt.

- Some of the advantages to marking **after** layering and basting include: less chance of having to re-mark and more freedom to adjust your design as you go. One disadvantage is that you have to mark around your pins.

- One advantage to marking **before** layering and basting is that it is easier to draw on a single layer of fabric. Another advantage is that you can use a light box or table when tracing a template. The disadvantage is that some fabric marking tools will rub off before you can quilt the whole top.

Straight-Line Quilting

I always use tape for marking my quilt tops when doing simple straight-line quilting. If you choose to use a fabric marking pencil or marker, use a ruler or yardstick as a guide for drawing your quilting lines.

1. Decide which direction you want your quilting lines to go. I generally prefer the look of diagonal straight-line quilting but some quilts look better with vertical/horizontal stitching.
2. Decide on the spacing for your quilting lines. Taping and stitching are easier if you use a standard tape width, such as ½", 1", 1½", 2", etc.

> **tip** To help you visualize what your quilt top will look like when stitched, lay lengths of thread across your quilt top in a diagonal and then horizontal and vertical direction.

3. Depending on your chosen direction, place 2 pieces of tape in an x or +, through the center of the quilt (**Fig 11**).
4. Follow **The Utility Quilting Stitch**, page 72, to stitch along both long edges of the tape.
5. Reposition the pieces of tape a consistent distance from your first lines of stitching (**Fig. 12**).

Fig. 11

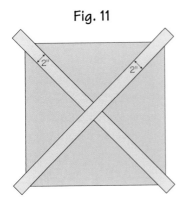

Fig. 12

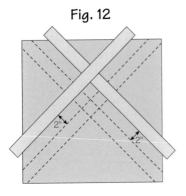

> **tip** If your rows are exactly the width of your tape you can stitch on both sides of the tape each time you move it. For example, if I am using 2" wide tape I move my tape over 2".

6. Stitch the next row(s). Continue moving the tape and stitching until you have quilted the entire quilt top. You may need to use new pieces of tape after several moves.

> **tip** I don't leave tape on a quilt for an extended period of time because it might leave a sticky residue on my quilt. But a few days or a couple weeks are usually ok. I try to tape a small area at a time. Tape is easy to put on so why take a chance of damaging the quilt by leaving it on.

Curved-Line Quilting

If you choose to quilt a curved-line design, such as a Baptist Fan, you will need to use a fabric marking pencil or marker and a template or stencil to mark your quilt top. Refer to **Marking Quilting Lines**, page 107, to trace a template or to make a stencil from a pattern.

TO HOOP OR NOT TO HOOP

I have quilted with and without a hoop and I much prefer **without** a hoop. I feel that it puts less strain on my wrists, it is more comfortable for me when stitching, and it's just more relaxing over all.

If you have never tried quilting without a hoop, I recommend that you stitch a small sample like a table runner or just a quilt sandwich made from scraps. See what you think! There is not a right or wrong way. Choose the method you prefer.

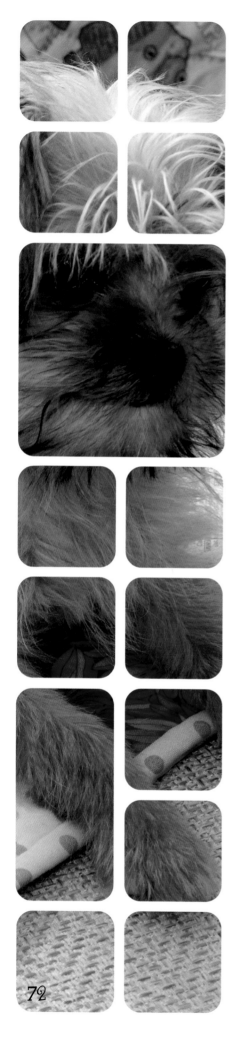

The Utility Quilting Stitch

The goal of Utility Quilting is to make a stitch that is about ⅛" long or 5-6 stitches per inch. Remember, this is not fine hand quilting — it should be fun and relaxing!

1. Thread your needle with an 18" - 20" length of thread; knot one end.
2. Using a thimble, insert the needle into the quilt top and batting (not through the backing) approximately 1" from where you plan to begin quilting. Bring the needle up through the quilt top on your quilting line (Fig. 13); when the knot catches on the quilt top, give the thread a quick, short pull to "pop" the knot through the fabric into the batting (Fig. 14).

Fig. 13	Fig. 14
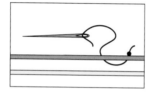	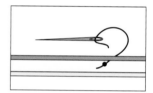

Note: When using floss, pearl cotton, and other heavy weight threads the knots will be harder to pop into the batting. If you can't get your knot to pop, you will need to start and stop your stitching on the back of your quilt. The knots will be seen and therefore become decorative elements!

tip When quilting, I stitch sideways from RIGHT to LEFT. Try this way first and if it doesn't feel comfortable, try a different direction. Some people like to stitch away and some like to stitch towards themselves.

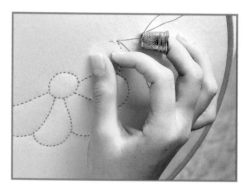

3. Holding the needle with your sewing hand and placing your other hand underneath the quilt, push the tip of the needle down through all layers (Fig. 15). As soon as the needle touches your underneath finger (usually the middle finger), use that finger to push the tip of the needle back up through the layers to the top of quilt.

4. Referring to Figs. 16-17, "rock" the needle up and down, loading three to six stitches on the needle before pulling the needle and thread completely through layers. Check the back of the quilt to make sure your stitches are going through all layers.

5. Every few stitches, tug very gently to pull the stitches FIRM. Not TIGHT, just FIRM. You don't want to pucker your quilting (Fig. 18).

tip For better control around curves and through seam allowances, I "stab stitch" one stitch at a time rather than "rocking" several stitches onto the needle.

6. At end of your thread, knot the thread close to the quilt surface and "pop" knot into batting; clip thread close to the quilt surface.

7. To continue the same line of quilting, start stitching with a new length of thread 1 stitch length away from where you ended.

Fig. 15

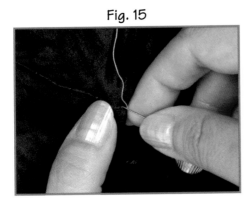

Fig. 16

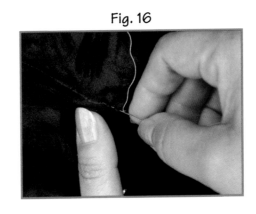

Fig. 17

Fig. 18

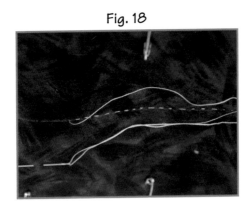

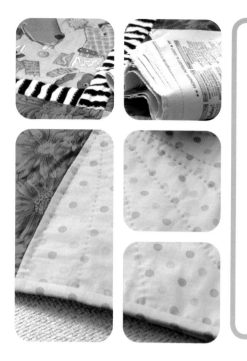

Puppies on Parade

To introduce you to Utility Quilting, I chose a very simple pieced design that will showcase your fabulous handwork! The bright, fun puppy fabric made this project such a joy to work on that I couldn't help but smile every time I picked it up to stitch!

Finished Quilt Size: 52" x 52" (132 cm x 132 cm)

FABRIC REQUIREMENTS

Yardage is based on 43"/44" (109 cm/112 cm) wide fabric.

- 1 yd (91 cm) of multi-color theme print
- $^1/_4$ yd (23 cm) of black/white stripe
- 1 yd (91 cm) of red print
- $^5/_8$ yd (57 cm) of green polka dot (includes binding)
- $3^1/_8$ yds (2.9 m) of backing fabric

You will also need:

- 56" x 56" (142 cm x 142 cm) square of batting
- See **Supplies**, page 66, for my list of special Utility Quilting supplies

CUTTING THE BACKGROUND AND BORDERS

*Follow **Rotary Cutting**, page 103, to cut fabric. Cut all strips from the selvage-to-selvage width of the fabric. All measurements include $^1/_4$" seam allowances.*

From multi-color theme print:
- Cut 1 **center square** $34^1/_2$" x $34^1/_2$".

From black/white stripe:
- Cut 2 **top/bottom inner borders** $1^1/_2$" x $34^1/_2$".
- Cut 2 **side inner borders** $1^1/_2$" x $36^1/_2$".

From red print:
- Cut 4 **outer borders** 8" x $36^1/_2$".

From green polka dot:
- Cut 4 **corner squares** 8" x 8".
- Cut 6 **binding strips** $1^1/_2$"w.

ASSEMBLING THE QUILT TOP

Follow **Piecing**, page 103, and **Pressing**, page 104, to assemble the quilt top. Refer to photo, page 76, for placement. Use $^1/_4$" seam allowances throughout.

1. Sew **top/bottom** and then **side inner borders** to **center square**.
2. Sew 2 **outer borders** to opposite sides of center square.
3. Sew 1 **corner square** to each end of each remaining outer border.
4. Sew remaining borders to center square to complete quilt top.

1. Follow **Utility Quilting**, page 66, to mark and quilt. My quilt is quilted with diagonal crosshatch quilting in the center square. There are widely-space parallel horizontal and vertical lines in the outer borders and a ray pattern in the corner squares.

3. Refer to **Making a Hanging Sleeve**, page 109, to make and attach a hanging sleeve, if desired.

4. Use **binding strips** and follow **Pat's Machine-Sewn Binding**, page 110, to bind quilt.

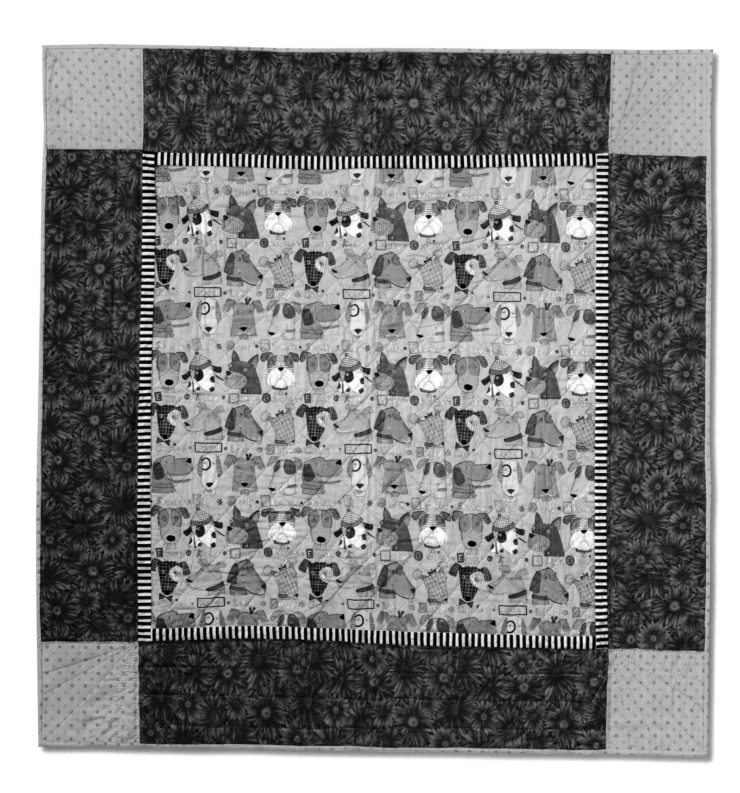

Trash Bag Quilts

I'm really inspired by the women, like our great-grandmothers, who quilted before us. Their "use it up, wear it out, make it do, or do without" attitude motivates me to be — what's the right word — frugal! AND, creating something useful and beautiful from scraps or "leftovers" is what a Trash Bag quilt is all about.

The difference between a scrap quilt and a Trash Bag quilt is in the construction. To make a scrap quilt, you cut your scraps into shapes like squares, triangles, etc., and then sew those shapes together into a block. To make a Trash Bag quilt, you sew your scraps together to make a new piece of "fabric", **and then** cut out blocks or shapes from the new fabric. You end up with very interesting, often unplanned, results.

Pictured below are two antique Trash Bag quilt tops from my collection. Notice all the odd fabric bits and shapes? They have been sewn together, then cut into blocks, and finally pieced into a quilt top. On pages 82-83 you will find several modern examples of Trash Bag Quilts.

Gathering the trash

Anyone who quilts produces fabric scraps. I keep a plastic trash bag clamped to my cutting table to collect my fabric scraps for later use. Most of us hang onto our scraps because we might *need* them someday. Well, today is the day! Grab your bag of scraps — we are going to make NEW FABRIC from our TRASH!

If you feel you may not have enough scraps in your trash bag or you just want more variety, you might want to go through your fabric stash and pull out some small fabric pieces (ones that are too big to be in your trash bag but smaller than a fat quarter). If you are still not sure that you have enough scraps, you can always ask your friends to share some of their trash.

Making New Fabric

I ADORE making new fabric! Making new fabric is mindless and your end result is fabulous ... what could be more rewarding? With this technique we will make large pieces of new fabric and then trim them to the size needed for your project.

Color Thoughts

While trash bag quilts are meant to be scrappy, with a little thought they can have a harmonized look.

- Dump your trash bag(s) out on your sewing table. I really *do* dump out my bag on a table or even sometimes on the floor!

- If I want a certain color theme for my quilt, I might sort the fabric by color.

- If your trash bag contains just scraps from your last quilt or last couple of quilts, you probably have lots of coordinating fabrics. Debbie's quilt, page 82, is an example of using coordinated scraps.

- If your trash bag contains scraps that you have had for years, you probably have fabrics in a wide array of colors like my **Beauty From Scraps** quilt, page 84.

- If your scraps contain a dominant color, you will want to use some of that color in as many different blocks as you can. Then that color will be scattered throughout your quilt.

- If you prefer to work mainly in one color family (such as red) include little bits of other colors such as gold, black, plum, or dark green to give the main color some interest. Peggy's quilt on page 83, is a good example of using one main color family.

- It's fun to include a spark of unexpected color, like a touch of yellow in each block.

- If you find that you don't have or don't want to use a dominant color or one color family, just go for pure scrappy randomness!

- You might find that you want to play around with several color combinations as you make your new fabric. It's a good thing that you have collected so much trash!

The Sewing Process

Making new fabric is really addictive. The students in my workshop did not want to stop making new fabric to make their quilts!

Fig. 1

1. Use a neutral color 100% cotton sewing thread in your machine and bobbin. **Note:** For photography purposes I used a high contrast thread.

2. Place your cutting mat, ruler, and rotary cutter close to your sewing machine. You will need to straighten the edges of your scraps in order to sew them together (If you appliqué, like me, not all your scraps will have straight edges).

3. Pick two "like-sized" scraps from your scrap pile. Straighten the edges, if needed. **Note:** Like-size does not mean they have to be the same size, just similar sizes.

Fig. 2

> **tip** Because really wide pieces of fabric do not add any visual interest to this style quilt, I usually trim my larger scraps to 5" wide or less.

4. Match right sides and sew the two scraps together to start your piece of new fabric (**Fig. 1**).

> **tip** I press my seam allowances in one direction. Also, it's easier to straighten the edges when your fabric is pressed.

Fig. 3

5. Pick up another scrap, straighten, if needed, and sew it to the new fabric (**Fig. 2**).

> **tip** You can add the scraps vertically or horizontally as desired. If you have lots of narrow strips, you may want to include some wider pieces for variety.

Fig. 4

6. When sewing several strips together, every so often straighten the shorter end and sew a strip to that end (**Figs. 3-4**).

7. Straightening edges as needed, continue adding scraps to your new fabric until it is a little larger than desired or the size called for in your project instructions. **Note:** I usually make my new fabric a little larger than what I *think* I will need. For example, if I will need to cut an 8" x 8" square from my new fabric, I make the new fabric approximately 10" x 10". Then I am always sure that I will have enough to allow for straightening and trimming and, if I choose, I can fussy cut the squares.

8. At this point, you may have a piece of new fabric that looks similar to the ones shown in **Fig. 5**.

> tip
> If you find that you have a long or wide rectangle in your new fabric, you can slice the rectangle in half and add a narrow strip through the center (**Fig. 6**).

> tip
> For a little variety when making new fabric, try sewing "log cabin" style around a square or rectangle (**Fig. 7**). I usually keep the size of this style new fabric between 8½" and 12" square. I feel that you start to lose the log cabin look with smaller or larger squares. The block in the top left-hand corner of Heidi's quilt, page 83, is an example of this type of piecing.

How Much New Fabric Will I Need?

Now that you understand the fabric making process, you might wonder how much new fabric you need to make:

- If you are going to be cutting squares, for example, to make my **Beauty From Scraps** quilt on page 84, you will need to make one piece of new fabric for each square called for in the project instructions.

- If you plan to cut shapes from your new fabric, like the star points in my quilt on page 82, you need to make a piece of new fabric that is large enough to cut out the shapes you need.

- After you have made a few (4 or 5) pieces of new fabric, stop making new fabric and follow **Using Your New Fabric** to cut a few squares or shapes. This will help you see how your fabric translates into blocks and how the blocks will look together in a quilt.

Fig. 5

Fig. 6

Fig. 7

Using Your New Fabric

Making Blocks

This is really fun! You will be cutting one square (block) or shape from each piece of new fabric and then getting to design with those blocks.

1. Trim your blocks to the size called for in your project instructions or the size you desire (Fig. 8) or cut out your shapes.

2. Arrange the blocks on a flat surface or place them on a design wall. Do they "need" anything to make them work together? For example, maybe you have used a pink fabric in a few blocks and those blocks look great! Pull out more pink and use it in a few more blocks. Do you need to use wider or narrower strips? Do you need more color variety?

3. Making fabric choices based on what you learned in Step 2, make the remaining new fabric you will need and then cut out the blocks or shapes to complete your project.

Pulling It Together

1. After all your blocks are made, it's time to find the right border fabric to pull the quilt design together and frame the blocks. Lay your blocks on top of your border options to see which fabric(s) works best with your blocks.

2. If you plan to turn your blocks on point, you'll need to choose fabric for the side and corner setting triangles. You can use one fabric like Debbie's quilt, page 82, or several different ones in the same color family like my **Beauty from Scraps** quilt, page 84.

3. Appliqués can add even more interest to your quilt like the flowers on Heidi's quilt, the words on Peggy's quilt, and the vase of tulips on my quilt (Figs. 9-11).

Fig. 8

Fig. 9

Fig. 10

Fig. 11

A Gallery of Trash Bag Quilts

Quilt designed and made by:
Debbie MacDougall Conway
Approximate Finished Size:
30" x 30" (76 cm x 76 cm)

Quilt designed and made by:
Pat Sloan
Approximate Finished Size:
34" x 34" (86 cm x 86 cm)

Want to learn more?

If you have enjoyed making new fabric and want to learn more about the process and other ways to use your new fabric, look for my *Crooked Cabin Quilts*, Leisure Arts leaflet #3874.

Quilt designed and made by:
Peggy McIntire
Approximate Finished Size:
18" x 18" (46 cm x 46 cm)

Quilt designed and made by:
Heidi Haynes
Approximate Finished Size:
62" x 62" (157 cm x 157 cm)

Beauty from Scraps

I had lots of teal scraps in my trash bag so I planned my blocks with that as my main color. I added lots of navy, black, red, and a few touches of gold.

After I made my blocks, I chose my fabrics for the setting triangles and the borders. By laying the blocks on top of different fabrics, I could see how each fabric would look with my blocks.

As a final touch, I added some little daisy appliqués. I fused and then machine blanket stitched them in place, but you could use any of the appliqué techniques in this book.

Finished Quilt Size: 43" x 43" (109 cm x 109 cm)
Finished Block Size: 7¹/₂" x 7¹/₂" (19 cm x 19 cm)

FABRIC REQUIREMENTS

Yardage is based on 43"/44" (109 cm/112 cm) wide fabric.

- Trash bag of fabric scraps
- ¹/₂ yd (46 cm) **total** of assorted red prints for setting triangles
- ¹/₄ yd (23 cm) of blue stripe for inner border
- ⁵/₈ yd (57 cm) of teal floral for outer border
- 2⁵/₈ yds (2.4 m) of backing fabric
- ³/₈ yd (34 cm) **total** of assorted red prints for binding
- Scraps of assorted teal and yellow print fabrics for appliqués

You will also need:

- 47" x 47" (119 cm x 119 cm) square of batting
- Paper-backed fusible web
- Stabilizer (optional)

CUTTING OUT THE PIECES

Follow **Rotary Cutting**, page 103, to cut fabric. Cut all strips from the selvage-to-selvage width of the fabric. All measurements include ¹/₄" seam allowances. Setting triangles are over-cut so that the blocks will "float."

From assorted red print fabrics:

- Cut at least 2 squares 12⁵/₈" x 12⁵/₈". Cut squares **twice** diagonally to make 8 **side setting triangles.***
- Cut at least 2 squares 6⁷/₈" x 6⁷/₈". Cut squares **once** diagonally to make 4 **corner setting triangles.***

From blue stripe fabric:

- Cut 2 **side inner borders** 1¹/₄" x 33¹/₂".
- Cut 2 **top/bottom inner borders** 1¹/₄" x 35".

From teal floral fabric:

- Cut 2 **side outer borders** 4¹/₂" x 35".
- Cut 2 **top/bottom outer borders** 4¹/₂" x 43", pieced if needed.

From assorted binding fabrics:

- Cut 1¹/₂" wide strips, piecing as needed to make 5¹/₄ yds of **binding. Note:** My strips vary from 3" to 40" in length.

* For more variety, cut more squares and put the extra triangles in your trash bag.

CUTTING THE APPLIQUÉS

Follow **Preparing Fusible Appliqués**, page 104, to cut appliqués using the patterns below.
From assorted teal print fabrics:
- Cut 76 **daisy petals**.

From assorted yellow print fabrics:
- Cut 12 **daisy centers**.

ASSEMBLING THE QUILT TOP CENTER

Follow **Piecing**, page 103, and **Pressing**, page 104, to assemble the quilt top. Refer to photo for placement. Use ¼" seam allowances throughout.
1. Follow **Trash Bag Quilts**, page 77, to make 13 **Trash Bag Blocks** 8" x 8" (20 cm x 20 cm).

2. Referring to **Assembly Diagram**, sew **setting triangles** and **Blocks** into diagonal **Rows**.
3. Sew Rows together to complete **quilt top center**. Square quilt top center to 33½" x 33½".

ADDING THE BORDERS

1. Matching centers and corners, sew **side inner borders** to quilt top center.
2. Matching centers and corners, sew **top/bottom inner borders** to quilt top.
3. Repeat Steps 1-2 to add outer **side**, **top**, and then **bottom outer borders** to quilt top.

Assembly Diagram

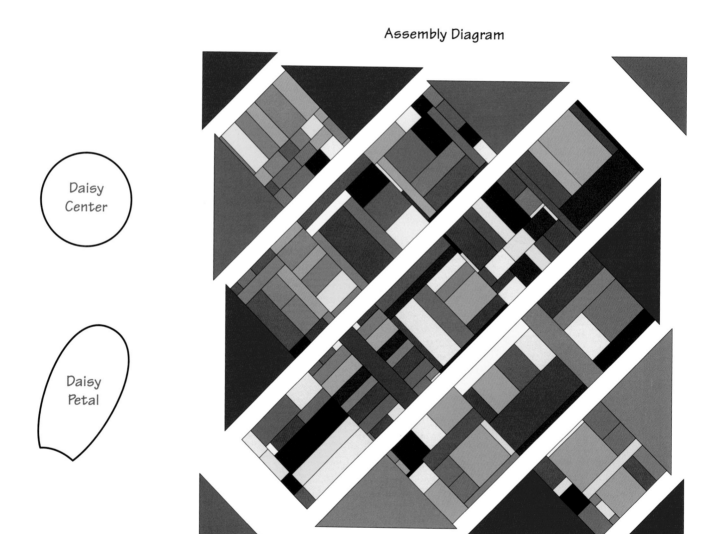

Daisy Center

Daisy Petal

ADDING THE APPLIQUÉS

Follow **Machine Blanket Stitch,** *page 105, to add appliqués.*

1. Appliqué 5 **daisy petals** and 1 **daisy center** on each corner setting triangle.
2. Appliqué 7 **daisy petals** and 1 **daisy center** on each side setting triangle.

FINISHING THE QUILT

1. Follow **Quilting**, page 106, to mark, layer, and quilt. My quilt is machine quilted with an all-over Baptist Fan pattern.
2. Refer to **Making a Hanging Sleeve**, page 109, to make and attach a hanging sleeve, if desired.
3. Use **binding** and follow **Steps 2-7** of **Pat's Machine-Sewn Binding**, page 110, to bind quilt.

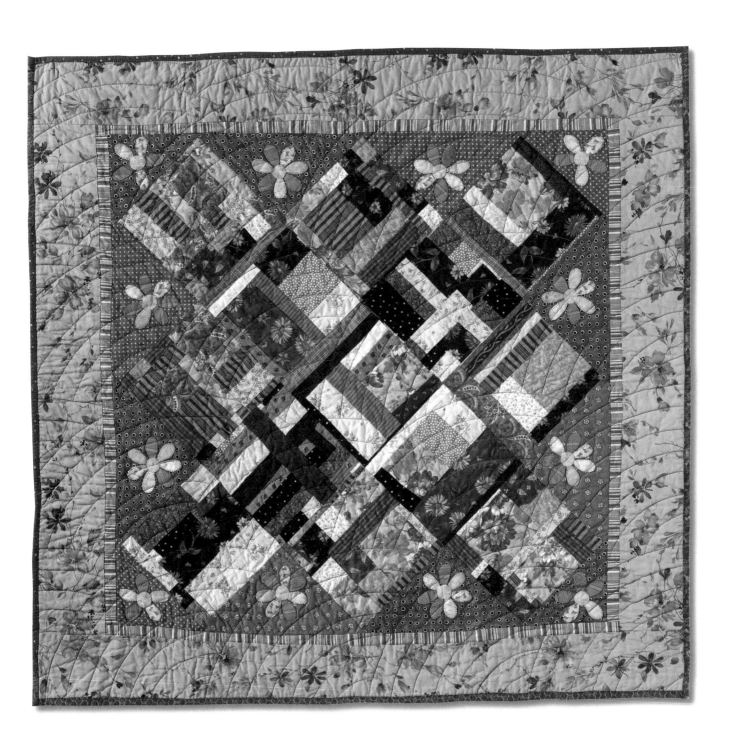

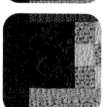

Calendar Quilts

Many years ago I started a calendar/memory quilt. The idea was to make a strip quilt by adding one fabric strip for every day of the year. The plan was to pick a fabric that was appropriate for the day, like a holiday fabric, a fabric that expressed my mood, or maybe one that I could write on to record the day's events or my feelings for that day.

I never finished that quilt but knew I loved the idea. So, last year I put out a challenge to my online quilting group to work with me all year on making calendar/memory quilts.

The guidelines were simple. The quilt did not have to cover a calendar year. It could be a record/memory quilt of any period of time. The deadline for completion was one year. Each participant was to make their quilt their own—do what spoke to them.

The resulting quilts, shown on pages 88-93, are just wonderful! You will notice that no two quilts are alike. One lady celebrated the first 100 days of her new granddaughter's life, some used lots of journaling, and one gal combined strips and pieced blocks. One quilt has a separate column for each month and another has wide sashings with appliquéd flowers. Each one is special and full of the memories of its creator.

Quilt designed and made by:
Keri Minnick
Approximate Finished Size:
50" x 93" (127 cm x 236 cm)

88

Planning Your Quilt

Are you ready to get started on your one-of-a-kind quilt? Although there are no hard and fast rules to follow when making a calendar/memory quilt, there are several questions you can ask yourself that will help you plan your quilt.

What style of quilt do I want to make?

- One style to consider is a "free-form" Chinese Coins quilt. With this style you add one strip of fabric for every day. The strips are cut approximately the same width but random heights. You can even use some triangular strips of fabric. My Year of Memories quilt, page 94, is an example of this style.

- Because not everyone wants to work in a random manner like I do, an "organized" Chinese Coins quilt might be just the style for you. You would still add one strip of fabric each day but the strips are all cut the exact same width and height. Karen's quilt, right, is a good example of this style.

- Maybe you like the idea of the Chinese Coins setting but feel that including some blocks might tell your story better than just using strips. Keri's quilt, opposite, combines an interesting mixture of strips and blocks.

- If you don't think you want to use strips at all, you might consider a Block of the Month style quilt. Can you actually use 365 different pieces of fabric in a block quilt? Maybe, maybe not — the challenge here will be to actually MAKE one block a month.

Quilt designed and made by:
Karen Martin
Approximate Finished Size:
63" x 90" (160 cm x 229 cm)

What period of time do I want to cover?

Depending on the number of days in your chosen time period, the number of strips you put in each column and the number of columns you use will vary.

- You may want to make a quilt that covers an entire calendar year.

- You may choose to concentrate on a specific period of time such as a school year or the first six months of a grandchild's life.

How do I know what size to make my quilt?

The exciting thing about this type of quilt is that it can be any size you desire. The dimensions of the strips, the number of strips in each column, the width of the columns and the width of the sashings/borders are all up to you! The examples below may help you to make those decisions.

- One approach is to first decide on the number of columns you want in your quilt and how many strips you want in each column. For example, let's say you want to make an "organized" Chinese Coins quilt that covers a calendar year. And you want your quilt to have 7 columns with 52 strips in each column, which equals 364 days (use the last strip of the year to make a label). If each strip is 8" x 1½", finished, your finished columns would measure 8" x 78". Add 4" wide, finished, sashings and borders and your finished quilt size would be 76" x 88".

Quilt designed and made by:
Mary Ellen Little
Approximate Finished Size:
57" x 73" (145 cm x 185 cm)

- Another option that works for either a "free-form" or "organized" Chinese Coins quilt is to start with a quilt size. For example, let's say you want your quilt to be approximately 90" x 91". You want a quilt that covers a whole year. You want each column to cover a 3-month period or approximately 91 days, so you will need 4 columns. You want a sashing strip between each column and two side borders. That gives you 4 columns, 3 sashing strips, and 2 borders across the width of your quilt for a total of 9 vertical sections. Divide 9 into your desired width of 90" and each column, sashing and border would be 10" wide, finished.

  To figure the height of each strip, you would divide the 91 strips into the desired quilt length of 91". The finished height of each strip would be 1" for an "organized" quilt. For a free-form quilt, 1" is an **average**, the strips will be random sizes and just need to **total** 91" when sewn together. Verity's quilt on page 92 is a good example of an "organized" version of this type quilt.

- My last suggestion is to let the quilt be whatever size it wants to be. For example, let's say you are recording a calendar year. You might want each column to cover a 2 month period so you are going to need 6 columns. Column 1 (Jan. and Feb.) depending on the year, would have 59 or 60 strips. Column 2 (March and April) would have 61, etc. After you make Column 1, measure it. Adjust your strip height, as needed, in the remaining columns so that they will be the same length as Column 1. You would cut your sashing strips and side borders the length of your columns x the width you desire. Your top and bottom borders would be cut the width of your quilt top center.

Quilt designed and made by:
Cathy Leitner
Approximate Finished Size:
68" x 94" (173 cm x 239 cm)

MORE OPTIONS

Now that you have a plan for your quilt, here are few suggestions to get you thinking about ways to make this quilt totally YOU!

- Pick a different color theme for each month. For example, use blue for January, red for February, green for March, etc.

- Use one tone-or-tone or light solid strip each month for journaling.

- Separate the months with a wide strip and appliqué the name of the month on this strip.

- Use novelty prints for special occasions.

- Add ribbons, charms, specialty fibers, or photo transfers to embellish your quilt.

- Use an embroidery machine to create special motifs.

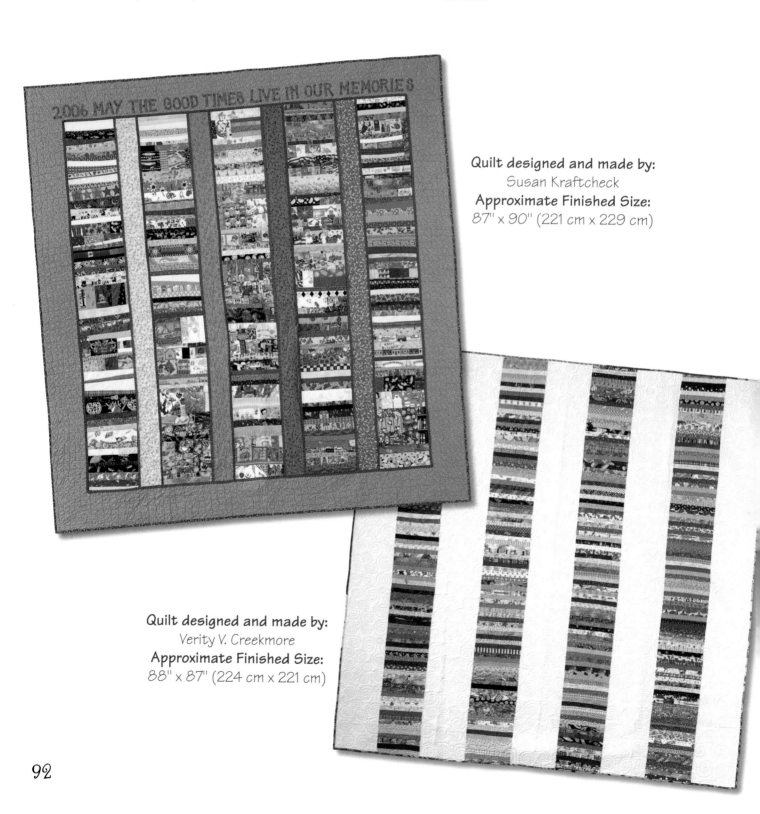

Quilt designed and made by:
Susan Kraftcheck
Approximate Finished Size:
87" x 90" (221 cm x 229 cm)

Quilt designed and made by:
Verity V. Creekmore
Approximate Finished Size:
88" x 87" (224 cm x 221 cm)

- Make the quilt as a gift. Select fabrics that remind you of the recipient. Journal information about their life on the strips.

- Sew 3 or 4 small pieces of fabric together to make one strip. It can count as 3 or 4 days.

- Appliqués can be counted as a day's addition, if desired. I counted each appliquéd letter from the month names as a separate day.

- Let your months flow from one column to the next. You don't have to begin and end a column with the first or last day of a month.

- Narrow sashing strips make the columns stand out more.

- Wide sashing strips provide a place to add appliqué or fancy quilting.

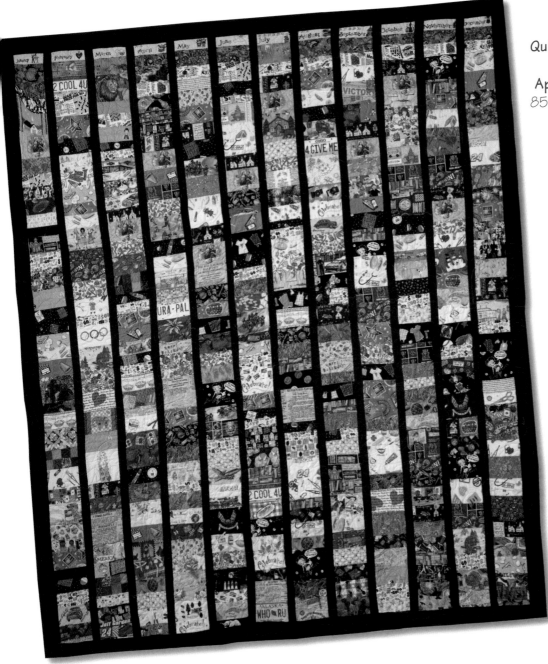

Quilt designed and made by:
Mary Eloise Sarsfield
Approximate Finished Size:
85" x 98" (216 cm x 249 cm)

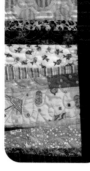

A Year in Memories

I chose to use a "free-form" Chinese Coin setting and followed my original idea of adding a new strip or appliqué each day.

Finished Quilt Size: 57" x 73" (145 cm x 185 cm)

FABRIC REQUIREMENTS

Yardage is based on 43"/44" (109 cm/112 cm) wide fabric.

- 1³/₄ yds (1.6 m) of green/black stripe
- Assorted fabric scraps (includes binding)
- 4¹/₂ yds (4.1 m) of backing fabric

You will also need:

- 64" x 80" (163 cm x 203 cm) rectangle of batting
- Paper-backed fusible web
- Fine-point permanent fabric marker (optional for journaling)

CUTTING THE PIECES

*Follow **Rotary Cutting**, page 103, to cut fabric. Cut all strips from the selvage-to-selvage width of the fabric. All measurements include ¹/₄" seam allowances.*

From green/black stripe:

- Cut 3 **sashing strips** 4¹/₂" x 64¹/₂", piecing as needed.
- Cut 2 **side borders** 4¹/₂" x 64¹/₂", piecing as needed.
- Cut 2 **top/bottom borders** 4¹/₂" x 56¹/₂", piecing as needed.

From assorted fabric scraps:

- Cut 1¹/₂" wide strips, piecing as needed to make 7¹/₂ yds of **binding**. **Note:** My strips are all peach/rust prints and vary from 4" to 28" in length.

ASSEMBLING THE QUILT TOP

*Follow **Piecing**, page 103, and **Pressing**, page 104, to assemble the quilt top. Use ¹/₄" seam allowances throughout. Refer to **Machine Appliqué**, page 104, to use alphabet patterns, page 96.*

1. On Day 1, select the first fabric for column 1. Cut the strip 9¹/₂" wide x desired height. **Note:** When cutting your strips, keep in mind that the target height for each column is 64¹/₂".
2. On Day 2, and on each following day, sew a new strip or appliqué to column 1. **Note:** Measure your column each week and adjust the height of your strips as needed to reach the target height.
3. After you have reached 64¹/₂" start a new column. Make 4 columns.

Adding the sashings and borders

1. Sew 4 columns and 3 **sashing** strips together to make **quilt top center**.
2. Sew 1 **side border** to each side of quilt top center.
2. Sew 1 **top/bottom border** to top and bottom edges of quilt top center to make **quilt top**.

FINISHING THE QUILT

1. Follow **Quilting**, page 106, to mark, layer, and quilt. My quilt is machine quilted with an allover leaf and flower pattern.
2. Refer to **Making a Hanging Sleeve**, page 109, to make and attach a hanging sleeve, if desired.
3. Use **binding** and follow **Steps 2-7** of **Pat's Machine-Sewn Binding**, page 110, to bind quilt.

JAN

FEB

MAR

APR

MAY

JUN

JUL

AUG

SEPT

OCT

NOV

DEC

Stamping Labels

I love using stamps for my paper crafting projects and wanted to find a way to incorporate them into my quilting. I decided that stamping on my quilt labels was the perfect way to combine the two crafts. Adding a stamped design to a plain label takes it from ordinary to extraordinary! Plus it's fun and easy to do—what could be better than that?

Supplies

I use two types of stamps, foam and rubber, and each has its own special supplies. You may have some of these already in your "craft closet" and the rest are readily available in most craft stores.

Foam Stamping:

- **Foam Stamps** – These stamps are easy to use and the designs are usually very simple. You won't find as large a selection as you will with rubber stamps but they are a good bit less expensive.

- **Acrylic Paints** – I use acrylic paints with my foam stamps. I like the fact that the stamped images have a richer color with paint than with ink. Acrylic paints come in a huge variety of colors, are easy to find, and are inexpensive. Clean up is quick and easy with just water.

- **Fabric Painting Medium** – I use this with my acrylic paints to soften and thin the paint which makes it adhere better to fabric.

- **Plastic Plates** – These are handy for mixing the paint and fabric medium.

Foam Stamping Supplies

Rubber Stamping Supplies

- **Foam Brushes** – Use these to apply the paint to the foam stamps. The 1" wide size works fine.

- **Water Container** – I keep an old glass canning jar handy for rinsing my foam brushes.

Rubber Stamping:
- **Rubber Stamps** – These stamps usually have a wooden or acrylic base. There are hundreds of designs to choose from. I usually stay away from extremely detailed stamps because the details get lost on fabric.

- **Inkpads** – The colors are usually softer and more muted than paint. I especially like Tim Holtz™ Distress Inks™ by Ranger Industries and VersaMagic™ by Tsunkineko®, Inc. These don't say that they are designed for use on fabric but I have good success with them. If you will be washing your quilt, look for inkpads labeled permanent on fabric.

- **Baby Wipes** – These work great for cleaning the ink off my rubber stamps.

You will also need:
- Squares or rectangles of light color 100% cotton fabric for labels (8" x 8" is a handy size)

- Scraps of light color 100% cotton fabric (for practicing)

- White paper (for practicing and blotting excess paint or ink)

- Paper towels

Foam Stamping

Fig. 1

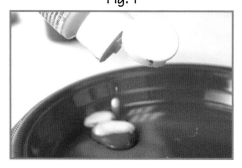

Fig. 2

1. Follow the manufacturer's directions to mix fabric medium into your paint (**Fig. 1**).
2. Use your foam brush to lightly apply the paint to the foam stamp (**Fig. 2**). Try to keep the paint on the raised surfaces and avoid letting it build up in the crevices.

   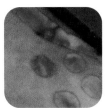

3. To stamp a test on a piece of white paper, place the stamp, painted side down on the paper. Press at the center of the stamp, pushing the stamp straight down. Press firmly and don't rock the stamp. If you rock, the edges of the stamp may touch the paper and leave unwanted lines. Lift the stamp straight up (**Figs. 3-5**).

4. Now try a test on a scrap of fabric (**Fig. 6**). Is there too much paint? "Stamp off" any excess paint onto white paper. Is there too little paint? Reapply paint to the stamp.

5. Continue practicing until you feel comfortable knowing exactly how much paint to apply to your stamp to achieve the look you want without having to continually "stamp off" and reapply. Also, practice the amount of pressure to use when pressing your stamp onto the fabric.

6. When you are ready, apply paint and stamp on your label. Let it dry completely.

7. Using a pressing cloth and a dry iron set to "cotton", heat set the paint by pressing the design for a few seconds.

Clean up

1. Use water to rinse the paint out of your foam brush.

    tip If your brush is really icky, throw it out. Foam brushes are very inexpensive and usually don't last very long.

2. Rinse your foam stamps under running water. Let them air dry completely before putting them away.

    tip To make your labels even more unique, use a fine-point permanent fabric marker to record any desired information on your labels. Add borders in fabrics that match your quilt or embellishments like beads, buttons, ribbons, etc.

Fig. 3

Fig. 4

Fig. 5

Fig. 6

Rubber Stamping

Fig. 7

Fig. 8
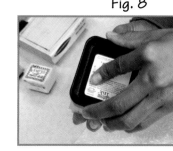

Fig. 9

Fig. 10
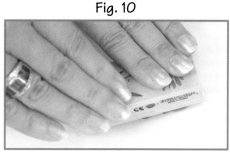
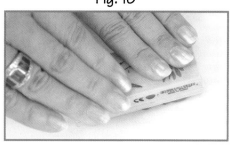

Fig. 11
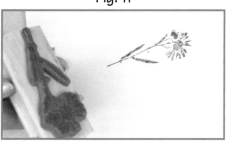

Fig. 12
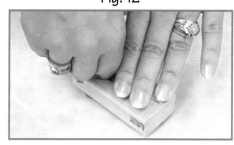

Fig. 13
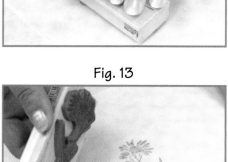

1. Hold the stamp in your hand with the image facing up. Pat the inkpad on the stamp (**Figs. 7-8**). You get better ink coverage when you apply the ink to the stamp rather than pushing the stamp down on the inkpad.

2. To stamp a test on a piece of white paper, place the stamp, inked side down on the paper. Press at the center of the stamp, pushing the stamp straight down. Press firmly and don't rock the stamp. If you rock, the edges of the stamp may touch your fabric and leave unwanted lines. Lift the stamp straight up (**Figs. 9-11**).

3. Now try a test on a scrap of fabric (**Figs. 12-13**). Is there too much ink? "Stamp off" any excess ink onto white paper. Is there too little ink? Reapply ink to the stamp.

4. Continue practicing until you feel comfortable knowing exactly how much ink to apply to your stamp to achieve the look you want without having to continually "stamp off" and reapply. Also, practice the amount of pressure to use when pressing your stamp onto the fabric.

5. When you are ready, apply ink and stamp on your label. Let it dry completely.

6. After you have finished with a color, "stamp off" any excess ink onto a piece of white paper (Fig. 14).

tip I like to save my stamped practice pieces of white paper to use when making cards. I cut out the images and use them to decorate my cards.

7. Using a pressing cloth and a dry iron, heat set the ink by pressing the label for a few seconds.

Clean up

1. Clean your rubber stamps by wiping them with baby wipes until no ink remains on the stamps (Fig. 15).

2. Stamp off any extra cleaning liquid onto a paper towel.

3. Let the stamps air dry completely before putting them away.

tip If you are REALLY into stamping, buy a big box of wipes. Put the stamps, rubber side down, on top of the stack of wipes and rub until clean. Throw away used wipe and repeat until stamp is clean. Clean up is all neat and tidy!

tip I keep my container of wipes in a re-sealable plastic bag so they won't dry out.

Fig. 14

Fig. 15

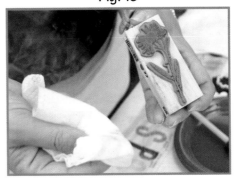

Beyond Labels

Stamping on fabric is not just limited to labels on the back of a quilt. I have a few suggestions for taking your new-found stamping skills to the FRONT of a project!

- Alternate stamped blocks with pieced blocks in your quilt.

- Combine stamping and appliqué in the same block.

- Stamp words or a quote in a border or on a block—it's much faster than appliqué or embroidery!

- Use stamped designs on the front of a purse or tote.

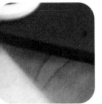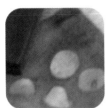

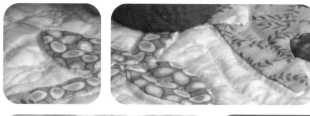
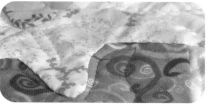
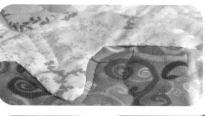

General Instructions

To make your quilting easier and more enjoyable, we encourage you to carefully read all of the general instructions, study the color photographs, and familiarize yourself with the individual project instructions before beginning a project.

Fabrics

SELECTING FABRICS

Choose high-quality, medium-weight 100% cotton fabrics. All-cotton fabrics hold a crease better, fray less, and are easier to quilt than cotton/polyester blends.

Yardage requirements listed for each project are based on 43"/44" wide fabric with a "usable" width of 40" after shrinkage and trimming selvages. Actual usable width will probably vary slightly from fabric to fabric. Our recommended yardage lengths should be adequate for occasional re-squaring of fabric when many cuts are required.

PREPARING FABRICS

We recommend that all fabrics be washed, dried, and pressed before cutting. If fabrics are not pre-washed, washing the finished quilt will cause shrinkage and give it a more "antiqued" look and feel. Bright and dark colors, which may run, should always be washed before cutting. After washing and drying fabric, fold lengthwise with wrong sides together and matching selvages.

Rotary Cutting

Rotary cutting has brought speed and accuracy to quiltmaking by allowing quilters to easily cut strips of fabric and then cut those strips into smaller pieces.

- Place fabric on work surface with fold closest to you.

- Cut all strips from the selvage-to-selvage width of the fabric unless otherwise indicated in project instructions.

- Square left edge of fabric using rotary cutter and rulers (**Figs. 1 - 2**).

- To cut each strip required for a project, place ruler over cut edge of fabric, aligning desired marking on ruler with cut edge; make cut (**Fig. 3**).

- When cutting several strips from a single piece of fabric, it is important to make sure that cuts remain at a perfect right angle to the fold; square fabric as needed.

Fig. 1	Fig. 2	Fig. 3
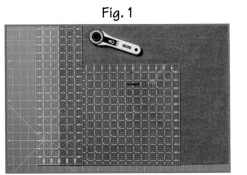	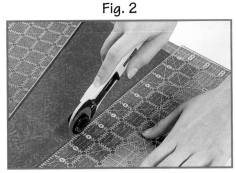	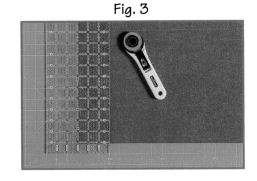

Piecing

- Set sewing machine stitch length for approximately 11 stitches per inch.

- Use neutral-colored general-purpose sewing thread (not quilting thread) in needle and in bobbin.

- An accurate 1/4" seam allowance is essential. Presser feet that are 1/4" wide are available for most sewing machines.

- When piecing, always place pieces right sides together and match raw edges; pin if necessary.

- Chain piecing saves time and will usually result in more accurate piecing.

- Trim away points of seam allowances that extend beyond edges of sewn pieces.

SEWING ACROSS SEAM INTERSECTIONS
When sewing across intersection of two seams, place pieces right sides together and match seams exactly, making sure seam allowances are pressed in opposite directions (**Fig. 4**).

SEWING SHARP POINTS
To ensure sharp points when joining triangular or diagonal pieces, stitch across the center of the "X" (shown in pink) formed on wrong side by previous seams (**Fig. 5**).

Fig. 4	Fig. 5
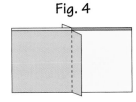	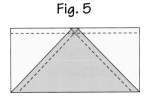

Pressing

- Use steam iron set on "Cotton" for all pressing.

- Press after sewing each seam.

- Seam allowances are almost always pressed to one side, usually toward darker fabric. However, to reduce bulk it may occasionally be necessary to press seam allowances toward the lighter fabric or even to press them open.

- To prevent dark fabric seam allowance from showing through light fabric, trim darker seam allowance slightly narrower than lighter seam allowance.

- To press long seams, such as those in long strip sets, without curving or other distortion, lay strips across width of the ironing board.

Machine Appliqué

Fig. 6

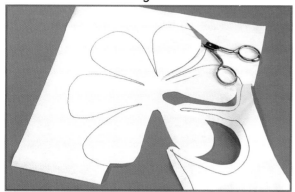

Fig. 7

PREPARING FUSIBLE APPLIQUÉ

*Machine appliqué patterns are printed in reverse and you **do not** need to add seam allowances. This to enables you to use this speedy method of preparing fusible appliqués.*

*tip Sometimes you may find instructions that call for a pattern to be cut in reverse. This is because the shape will be used facing both directions. Use a black fine-point marker to trace the pattern onto plain white paper, flip the paper over, and then follow **Steps 1 – 4** to trace pattern onto web from the "wrong" side of the paper.*

1. Place paper-backed fusible web, web side down, over appliqué pattern. Use a pencil to trace pattern onto paper side of web as many times as indicated in project instructions for a single fabric. Repeat for additional patterns and fabrics.

2. To reduce stiffness when appliquéing, cut away the center of the fusible web ¼" inside the traced line. Do not cut on the line (Fig. 6). It may not be necessary to cut away the center of small or narrow pieces.

3. Follow manufacturer's instructions to fuse traced patterns to wrong side of fabrics. Do not remove paper backing.

4. Cut out appliqué pieces along traced lines (Fig. 7). Remove paper backing from all pieces.

MACHINE BLANKET STITCH

*Some sewing machines feature a Blanket Stitch similar to the one I used for my **Beauty From Scraps** quilt, page 84. Refer to your owner's manual for machine set-up. If your machine does not have this stitch, try any of the decorative stitches your machine has until you are satisfied with the look.*

1. Thread sewing machine and bobbin with 100% cotton thread.

    tip Matching the thread color to the appliqué will make the stitches just disappear. Using contrasting thread will make your stitches stand out as a design element.

2. Attach an open-toe presser foot. Select far right needle position and needle down (if your machine has these features).

3. If desired, spray the wrong side of your background (quilt top) 3 or 4 times with starch, ironing dry between applications. This gives the fabric enough stability that it won't bunch up while stitching.

4. Position quilt top under presser foot where you will begin stitching. Bring bobbin thread to the top of the fabric by lowering then raising the needle, bringing up the bobbin thread loop. Pull the loop all the way to the surface.

5. Begin by stitching 5 or 6 stitches in place (drop feed dogs or set stitch length at 0), or use your machine's lock stitch feature, if equipped, to anchor thread. Return setting to selected Blanket Stitch.

6. Most of the Blanket Stitch should be done on the appliqué with the right edges of the stitch falling at the very outside edge of the appliqué. Stitch over all exposed raw edges of appliqué pieces.

7. (**Note:** Dots on **Figs. 10 – 14** indicate where to leave needle in fabric when pivoting.) Always stopping with needle down in background fabric, refer to **Fig. 10** to stitch outside points like tips of leaves. Stop one stitch short of point. Raise presser foot. Pivot project slightly, lower presser foot, and make one angled **Stitch 1**. Take next stitch, stop at point, and pivot so **Stitch 2** will be perpendicular to point. Pivot slightly to make **Stitch 3**. Continue stitching.

8. For outside corners (**Fig. 11**), stitch to corner, stopping with needle in background fabric. Raise presser foot. Pivot project, lower presser foot, and take an angled stitch. Raise presser foot. Pivot project, lower presser foot and stitch adjacent side.

9. For inside corners (**Fig. 12**), stitch to the corner, taking the last bite at corner and stopping with the needle down in background fabric. Raise presser foot. Pivot project, lower presser foot, and take an angled stitch. Raise presser foot. Pivot project, lower presser foot and stitch adjacent side.

Fig. 10

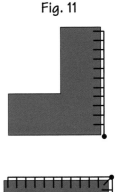

Fig. 11

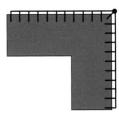

Fig. 12

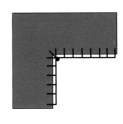

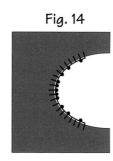

Fig. 13 **Fig. 14**

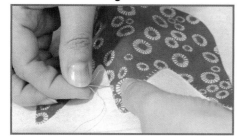

Fig. 15

10. When stitching outside curves (**Fig. 13**), stop with needle down in background fabric. Raise presser foot and pivot project as needed. Lower presser foot and continue stitching, pivoting as often as necessary to follow curve. Small circles may require pivoting between each stitch.

11. When stitching inside curves (**Fig. 14**), stop with needle down in background fabric. Raise presser foot and pivot project as needed. Lower presser foot and continue stitching, pivoting as often as necessary to follow curve.

12. When stopping stitching, use a lock stitch to sew 5 or 6 stitches in place or use a needle to pull threads to wrong side of background fabric (**Fig. 15**); knot, then trim ends.

Quilting

*Quilting holds the three layers (top, batting, and backing) of the quilt together and can be done by hand or machine. Because marking, layering, and quilting are interrelated and may be done in different orders depending on circumstances, please read entire **Quilting** section, pages 106 – 109, before beginning project.*

TYPES OF QUILTING DESIGNS

In the Ditch Quilting
Quilting along seamlines or along edges of appliquéd pieces is called "in the ditch" quilting. This type of quilting should be done on side opposite seam allowance and does not have to be marked.

Outline Quilting
Quilting a consistent distance, usually 1/4", from seam or appliqué is called "outline" quilting. Outline quilting may be marked, or 1/4" masking tape may be placed along seamlines for quilting guide. (Do not leave tape on quilt longer than necessary, since it may leave an adhesive residue.)

Motif Quilting
Quilting a design, such as a feathered wreath, is called "motif" quilting. This type of quilting should be marked before basting quilt layers together.

Echo Quilting
Quilting that follows the outline of an appliquéd or pieced design with two or more parallel lines is called "echo" quilting. This type of quilting does not need to be marked.

Channel Quilting
Quilting with straight, parallel lines is called "channel" quilting. This type of quilting may be marked or stitched using a guide.

Crosshatch Quilting
Quilting straight lines in a grid pattern is called "crosshatch" quilting. Lines may be stitched parallel to edges of quilt or stitched diagonally. This type of quilting may be marked or stitched using a guide.

Meandering Quilting
Quilting in random curved lines and swirls is called "meandering" quilting. Quilting lines should not cross or touch each other. This type of quilting does not need to be marked.

MARKING QUILTING LINES

Quilting lines may be marked using fabric marking pencils, chalk markers, water- or air-soluble pens, or lead pencils.

Caution: Pressing may permanently set some marks. Test different markers on scrap fabric to find one that marks clearly and can be thoroughly removed.

Simple quilting designs, such as straight lines, may be marked with chalk or chalk pencil after basting. A small area may be marked, then quilted, before moving to next area to be marked.

Curved-line or intricate quilting designs can be marked before basting by tracing a pattern, or after basting by making a stencil from a pattern. A wide variety of pre-cut quilting stencils, as well as entire books of quilting patterns, are available.

To Mark Before Layering And Basting:

1. Make a copy of the pattern, reducing or enlarging the pattern as desired to fit your quilt. Use a black permanent marker to draw over the lines to make tracing easier.
2. Place the pattern on a flat surface (for light fabrics) or a light box (for dark fabrics).
3. Using a fabric marking tool, trace the pattern onto the quilt top. Move the quilt top as needed until the entire quilt top is marked.

To Mark After Layering And Basting:

1. To make a stencil from the pattern, center template plastic over pattern and use a permanent marker to trace pattern onto plastic. Use a craft knife with single or double blade to cut channels along traced lines (**Fig. 16**).
2. Place the quilt top on a flat surface. Position stencil where desired on the quilt top.
3. Using a fabric marking tool and following the cut channels of the stencil, draw the design onto the quilt top. Move stencil as needed to mark the next area. ***Note:*** I usually only mark a small area at a time, quilt that, and then mark the next area. If you wish to mark the entire quilt top, continue moving the stencil and drawing until marking is complete.

PREPARING THE BACKING

To allow for slight shifting of quilt top during quilting, backing should be approximately 2" to 4" larger on all sides. Yardage requirements listed for quilt backings are calculated for 43"/44"w fabric. Using 90"w or 108"w fabric for the backing may eliminate piecing. To piece a backing using 43"/44"w fabric, use the following instructions.

1. Measure length and width of quilt top; add 8" (4" for smaller quilts or wall hangings) to each measurement.
2. Cut backing fabric into two lengths slightly longer than determined length measurement. Trim selvages. Place lengths with right sides facing and sew long edges together, forming tube (**Fig. 17**). Match seams and press along one fold (**Fig. 18**). Cut along pressed fold to form single piece (**Fig. 19**).
3. Trim backing to size determined in **Step 1**; press seam allowances open.

Fig. 16

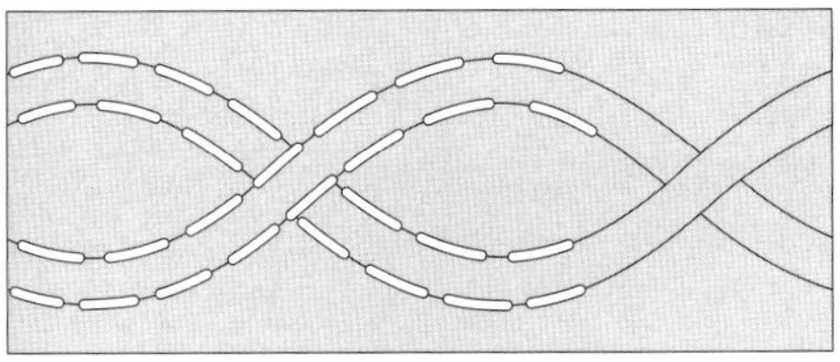

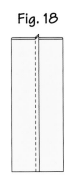

Fig. 17

Fig. 18

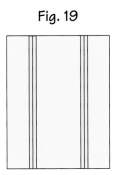

Fig. 19

107

CHOOSING THE BATTING

The appropriate batting will make quilting easier. For fine hand quilting, choose low-loft batting. All cotton or cotton/polyester blend battings work well for machine quilting because the cotton helps "grip" quilt layers. If quilt is to be tied, a high-loft batting, sometimes called extra-loft or fat batting, may be used to make quilt "fluffy."

Types of batting include cotton, polyester, wool, silk, cotton/polyester blend, and cotton/wool blend.

When selecting batting, refer to package labels for characteristics and care instructions. Cut batting same size as prepared backing.

ASSEMBLING THE QUILT

1. Examine wrong side of quilt top closely; trim any seam allowances and clip any threads that may show through front of the quilt. Press quilt top, being careful not to "set" any marked quilting lines.
2. Place backing wrong side up on flat surface. Use spring clamps or masking tape to secure the edges of backing to surface. Place batting on top of backing fabric. Smooth batting gently, being careful not to stretch or tear. Center quilt top right side up on batting.
3. Use 1" rustproof safety pins to "pin-baste" all layers together, spacing pins approximately 4" apart. Begin at center and work toward outer edges to secure all layers. If possible, place pins away from areas that will be quilted, although pins may be removed as needed when quilting.

MACHINE QUILTING METHODS
Straight-Line Quilting

The following instructions are for straight-line quilting, which requires a walking foot or even-feed foot. The term "straight-line" is somewhat deceptive, since curves (especially gentle ones) as well as straight lines can be stitched with this technique.

1. Using the same color general-purpose thread in the needle and bobbin avoids "dots" of bobbin thread being pulled to the surface.
2. Using general-purpose thread, which matches the backing in the bobbin, will add pattern and dimension to the quilt without adding contrasting color. Refer to your owner's manual for recommended tension settings.
3. Set stitch length for 6 to 10 stitches per inch and attach the walking foot to sewing machine.
4. After pin-basting, decide which section of the quilt will have the longest continuous quilting line, oftentimes the area from center top to center bottom. Leaving the area exposed where you will place your first line of quilting, roll up each edge of the quilt to help reduce the bulk, keeping fabrics smooth. Smaller projects may not need to be rolled.
5. Start stitching at beginning of longest quilting line, using very short stitches for the first 1/4" to "lock" quilting. Stitch across project, using one hand on each side of walking foot to slightly spread fabric and to guide fabric through machine. Lock stitches at end of quilting line.
6. Continue machine quilting, stitching longer quilting lines first to stabilize quilt before moving on to other areas.

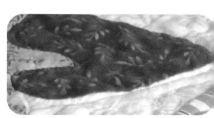

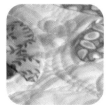

Free-Motion Quilting

Free-motion quilting may be free form or may follow a marked pattern.

1. Using the same color general-purpose thread in the needle and bobbin avoids "dots" of bobbin thread being pulled to the surface. Use general-purpose thread in the bobbin and decorative thread for stitching, such as metallic, variegated or contrasting-colored general-purpose thread, when you desire the quilting to be more pronounced.

2. Use a darning foot and lower or cover feed dogs. Pull up bobbin thread and hold both thread ends while you stitch 2 or 3 stitches in place to lock thread. Cut threads near quilt surface.

3. Place hands lightly on quilt on either side of darning foot to slightly spread fabric and to move fabric through the machine. Even stitch length is achieved by using smooth, flowing hand motion and steady machine speed. Slow machine speed and fast hand movement will create long stitches. Fast machine speed and slow hand movement will create short stitches. Move quilt sideways, back and forth, in a circular motion, or in a random motion to create desired designs; do not rotate quilt. Lock stitches at end of each quilting line.

Making a Hanging Sleeve

Attaching a hanging sleeve to back of wall hanging or quilt before the binding is added allows your project to be displayed on a wall.

1. Measure width of quilt top edge and subtract 1". Cut piece of fabric 7"w by determined measurement.

2. Press short edges of fabric piece 1/4" to wrong side; press edges 1/4" to wrong side again and machine stitch in place.

3. Matching wrong sides, fold piece in half lengthwise to form tube.

4. Before sewing binding to quilt, match raw edges and pin hanging sleeve to center top edge on back of quilt.

5. Bind quilt, treating hanging sleeve as part of backing.

6. Blindstitch bottom of hanging sleeve to backing, taking care not to stitch through to front of quilt.

Want to learn more?

Refer to my *Learn to Machine Quilt with Pat Sloan*, Leisure Arts leaflet #4596.

Pat's Machine-Sewn Binding

For a quick and easy finish when attaching straight-grain binding with overlapped corners, Pat sews her binding to the back of the quilt and Machine Blanket Stitches it in place on the front, eliminating all hand stitching.

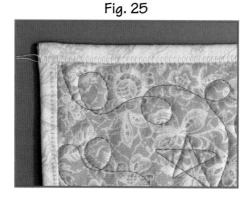

Fig. 20

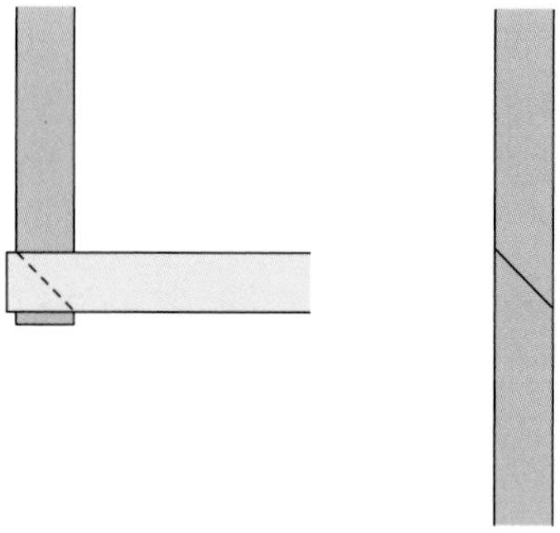

Fig. 21

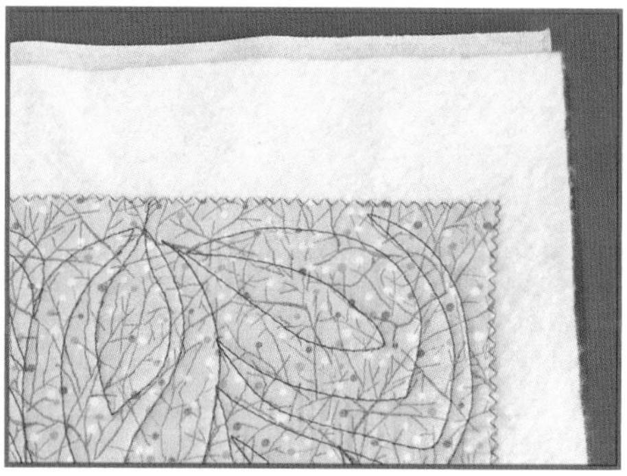

Fig. 22

Fig. 23

Fig. 24

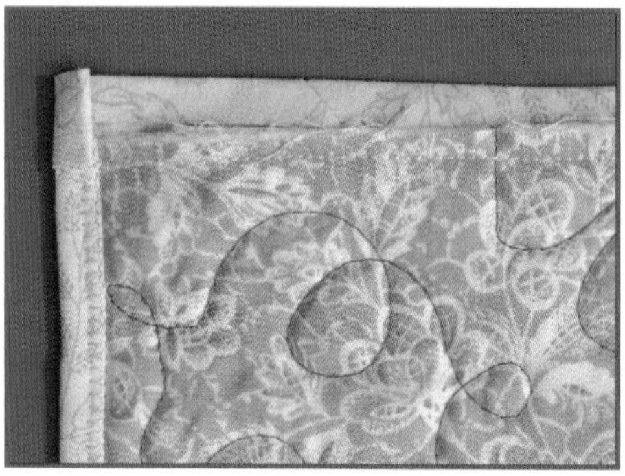

Fig. 25

1. With right sides together and using diagonal seams (**Fig. 20**), sew the short ends of binding strips together, if needed, to achieve the necessary length for each edge of quilt.
2. Press seam allowances open. Press one long edge of binding 1/4" to the wrong side.
3. Using a narrow zigzag or straight stitch, stitch around the quilt close to the raw edges (**Fig. 21**). Trim backing and batting even with edges of quilt top.
4. Matching raw edges and using a 1/4" seam allowance, sew binding to top and bottom edges on **back** side of the quilt.
5. Fold binding over to quilt front and pin pressed edges in place, covering stitching line (**Fig. 22**); Blanket Stitch or Top Stitch binding close to pressed edge. Trim ends of top and bottom binding even with edges of quilt top.
6. Leaving approximately 1 1/2" of binding at each end, stitch a length of binding to back side of each side of quilt (**Fig. 23**).
7. Trim each end of binding 1/2" longer than bound edge. Fold under each raw end of binding (**Fig. 24**); pin in place. Fold binding over to quilt front and Blanket Stitch or Topstitch in place (**Fig. 25**).

Signing and Dating Your Quilt

A completed quilt is a work of art and should be signed and dated. The label should reflect the style of the quilt, the occasion or person for which it was made, and the quilter's own particular talents. Making a stamped label, page 97, is one way to record a history of your quilt. Below are some other suggestions for making a special label for your quilt.

- Embroider quilter's name, date, and any additional information on quilt top or backing. Matching floss, such as cream floss on white border, will leave a subtle record. Bright or contrasting floss will make the information stand out.

- Make label from muslin and use a permanent marker to write information. Use different colored permanent markers to make label more decorative. Stitch label to back of quilt.

- Use photo-transfer paper to an add image to a white or cream fabric label. Stitch label to back of quilt.

- Piece an extra block from quilt top pattern to use as label. Add information with permanent fabric pen. Appliqué block to back of quilt.

- Write a message on an appliquéd design from quilt top. Attach appliqué to back of the quilt.

Metric Conversion Chart

Inches x 2.54 = centimeters (cm)			Yards x .9144 = meters (m)		
Inches x 25.4 = millimeters (mm)			Yards x 91.44 = centimeters (cm)		
Inches x .0254 = meters (m)			Centimeters x .3937 = inches (")		
			Meters x 1.0936 = yards (yd)		

		Standard Equivalents			
1/8"	3.2 mm	0.32 cm	1/8 yard	11.43 cm	0.11 m
1/4"	6.35 mm	0.635 cm	1/4 yard	22.86 cm	0.23 m
3/8"	9.5 mm	0.95 cm	3/8 yard	34.29 cm	0.34 m
1/2"	12.7 mm	1.27 cm	1/2 yard	45.72 cm	0.46 m
5/8"	15.9 mm	1.59 cm	5/8 yard	57.15 cm	0.57 m
3/4"	19.1 mm	1.91 cm	3/4 yard	68.58 cm	0.69 m
7/8"	22.2 mm	2.22 cm	7/8 yard	80 cm	0.8 m
1"	25.4 mm	2.54 cm	1 yard	91.44 cm	0.91 m

Thanks!

Thank you to P & B Textiles and Free Spirit fabric companies for providing many of the beautiful fabrics used in the projects for this book.

Thank you to Janome for providing the sewing machine I used for the workshop.

To make the projects I used Mettler® thread, Mountain Mist® batting, and HeatnBond Lite® fusible web.

Look for these and other Leisure Arts publications by Pat Sloan at your local retailer or shop online at theLeisureBoutique.com!

From beginner to advanced, Pat has a "how to" publication for you! Look for the School House logo for all your learning needs.

Leaflet #3649

Leaflet #4430

Leaflet #3784

Want to learn more?

Check out www.icantbelieveim.com for info on Pat's online quilting classes.

Sign up for our E-Newsletter at leisurearts.com. Contact us at 1-800-526-5111.

LEISURE ARTS®
the art of everyday living